Hot Off The Grill

BARBECUE RECIPES WITH AN ASIAN TOUCH

Carol Selva Rajah

mc Marshall Cavendish
Cuisine

The Publisher wishes to thank Aktif Lifestyle, Malaysia for the loan of their crockery and utensils and Meat & Lifestock Austrialia for sponsoring the meat supplies.

Chef's Assistants: Yvette Lee, Sivapakiam Sivapragasam and Michelle Thrift
Photographer: Jenhor Siow

© 2004 Marshall Cavendish International (Asia) Private Limited
First published 2004 as Celebrity Chefs' Cookbooks: Great Barbecues
This new edition 2009

Published by Marshall Cavendish Cuisine
An imprint of Marshall Cavendish International
1 New Industrial Road, Singapore 536196

Other Marshall Cavendish Offices:

Marshall Cavendish Ltd. 5th Floor, 32-38 Saffron Hill, London EC1N 8FH, UK • Marshall Cavendish Corporation. 99 White Plains Road, Tarrytown NY 10591-9001, USA • Marshall Cavendish International (Thailand) Co Ltd. 253 Asoke, 12th Flr, Sukhumvit 21 Road, Klongtoey Nua, Wattana, Bangkok 10110, Thailand • Marshall Cavendish (Malaysia) Sdn Bhd, Times Subang, Lot 46, Subang Hi-Tech Industrial Park, Batu Tiga, 40000 Shah Alam, Selangor Darul Ehsan, Malaysia

Marshall Cavendish is a trademark of Times Publishing Limited

National Library Board (Singapore) Cataloguing in Publication Data

Selva Rajah, Carol.
Hot off the grill : barbecue recipes with an Asian touch / Carol Selva Rajah. – New ed. – Singapore : Marshall Cavendish Cuisine, 2009.
p. cm.
ISBN-13 : 978-981-261-793-4
ISBN-10 : 981-261-793-0

1. Barbecue cookery. I. Title.

TX840.B3
641.76 -- dc22   OCN318309992

Printed in Singapore by Times Printers Pte Ltd

To Abel and Gomathy Arumugam for generously

opening their home to us so that the photography

for this book could be done.

CONTENTS

HAVING grown up with the television image of the Western male cook wielding a pair of tongs and wearing an apron to grill a few thick pieces of meat or fish on the barbecue, most young Asians think that barbecues originate from the West. In the West, the men take charge of the food for the Sunday afternoon lunch while the ladies make the salads and serve the drinks. This was the image of barbecues I had as a young girl when I first went to school in Australia – a memory of sizzling meat cooked by the men of the farm, wearing boots and heavy shirts, and sometimes an apron (which I found very odd).

There were no gas barbecues then. There were either coal or wood fired spits with a large metal barbecue plate sitting over the coals, on which a variety of meats sat cooking. There were no marinades used, again something that I found strange because in Malaysia, everything was cooked with some marinade or other. The marinade could be just a touch of soy sauce, lime juice or some oil.

But the concept is not foreign to us at all. All over Asia, we have also been grilling and barbecuing in our traditional styles for years although in a way that is quite different from the western barbecue. Who hasn't memories of the "old satay-man" with his charcoal grill, squatting nearby and fanning to keep the flame alive? The aromas that came from the tiny little burner never fail to evoke more memories than any other food stall from any of the markets. I remember such an old satay man, who used to charm us as much as his satay. He sold the best satay in town. And all he did was to grill his satay close to the old Port Klang railway station and to fan the flames while the faint burning and delicious smoking aromas wafted across the road, into the stores and into the library, tempting everyone in range.

There were not only satay stalls, but I also remember the gorgeous *Babi Guling* that we all tasted on our first visit to Bali and of course, the tempting aromas of grilled *Ikan Panggang*, served on the beaches of the east coast of Malaysia, and *Panggang Pari* or stingray fins grilled on small squares of banana leaf until the bones became brittle and melted into nothing.

Although we have used different methods of cooking with smaller pieces of meat and fish, Asians have always barbecued in traditional methods using smaller indoor and outdoor grills. Part of the reason for this may be because we seldom eat meat. Even when we do, we either cook it into stir-fries, adding meat to noodles with vegetables or we cook the pieces into curries. Therefore, we treat barbecuing in a similar manner, preferring to grill our meat in smaller pieces, and to season our meats and fish (as we do before stir-frying).

There are many methods that we could use to grill that would suit our purpose – small indoor grills that sit on the table, outdoor barbecues or smokeless grills that sit like overturned woks or *kuali*. The Japanese Hibachi grill is a popular method or one can use the heavy iron grilling plate that sits under an oven grill or over an open coal stove.

In India, the use of large Ali Baba-like clay jars called the tandoor, is well known and popular today in Indian restaurants all over the food world. This technique originated from the north of India, coming through the western frontier with the Moghul rulers, who were descendants of the Mongol hordes that swept across Asia and Europe. The Moghuls went to India and carved out an empire with their swords, cooking techniques and rich flavours and creamy sauces. The tandoor works on the principle that the clay jar is surrounded with bricks or sunk in the ground to give more insulation. Coals are lit at the bottom through an opening and the meats or fish are placed on spits and inserted into the oven to cook in the searing heat. To make traditional *naan* bread, flat discs of flour are placed against the walls of the tandoor to swell and cook in a classic teardrop shape. The reasons for using the jars are because earthenware imparts an earthy, smoky taste to the food and that the jars retain heat perfectly so that both the meat and the *naan* are cooked at the same time.

The Hindu Rajput rulers were great hunters. After hunting wild boar, they would dress the meat with ground turmeric, an antiseptic to preserve the meat until it was grilled on an open-air barbecue.

Barbecues may seem to be western in the minds of many but in actual fact, the West has adopted many of our Asian ways of cooking. The result is that this book is a blend of East and West, which reflects the exciting mix of different cuisines in Malaysia and Singapore.

So enjoy this book, remembering to change whatever that does not suit you or to adapt any recipe to another meat, for in the end, it is your palate, your family's tastes and your cooking that will bring the dish to life. The barbecue is an outdoor meal so gather your friends around you and have fun. But watch the meat and do not burn anything!

CAROL SELVA RAJAH

Butterflied Point Steaks with Sesame and Coconut *Kemangi* Sauce

Serves 4

This is a simple recipe using the best beef that you can buy and cooking it with ginger, pepper and sesame sauce. It is best served with coconut *kemangi* sauce (see pg 9).

INGREDIENTS
Meat
Beef steaks, eye fillet or rib eye steaks	4, each 80–100 g
Garlic	½ bulb

Marinade
Spring onions (scallions)	4, chopped
Ginger	2.5-cm knob, peeled and pounded
Garlic	2 cloves, peeled and pounded
Freshly ground black pepper	1 tsp
Sesame oil or olive oil	2 tsp

Note: Salt is only used at the end, just before serving, as it toughens meat when added while cooking.

METHOD
- Butterfly steaks (see pg 79). Using the blunt end of the knife, pound steaks to flatten.
- Combine spring onions, ginger, garlic, pepper and oil in a bowl. Brush on steaks and marinate covered for at least 1 hour in the refrigerator.
- The method allows for outdoor or indoor grilling.
- Drizzle some oil on ½ bulb garlic and grill with meat.
- See pg 79 for barbecue timings.

- To determine when steaks are done, look for a dark red colour and a smoky and garlic-roasted aroma. When steaks are done, sprinkle with salt, then leave to rest for 4–5 minutes.
- To serve, cut around bone to release meat. Slice across the grain into 5-mm slices and serve hot with warmed coconut *kemangi* sauce (see pg 9) or garlic aioli sauce with coriander (see pg 45) accompanied with a leafy green salad of lettuce, coriander leaves, roasted garlic and a light dressing of lime juice, palm sugar and salt or fish sauce.

Coconut Kemangi Sauce

Yields 250 ml

This sauce originated from East Java where coconut milk is commonly used. The mild spiciness, when combined with sweet basil, gives it a subtlety unseen in many other sauces. It goes well with lamb but may also be used with vegetables, prawns or fish.

INGREDIENTS

Light olive oil	1¹/₂ Tbsp
Shallots	4, peeled and diced
Garlic	3 cloves, peeled and diced
Red chillies	6, seeded and diced
Green chillies	3, seeded and diced
Thai sweet basil leaves (*kemangi*)	15, finely chopped + 1 sprig, torn into two so that aromas are released
Coconut milk	250 ml

METHOD

- Heat oil in a frying pan (skillet). Sauté shallots, garlic and chillies for 3–5 minutes without browning.
- Add in Thai basil leaves and coconut milk. Bring mixture to the boil, then reduce heat and simmer for 10 minutes.
- Pour into a blender and blend for 2–3 minutes at high speed until smooth.
- Pour mixture back into saucepan. Stir in torn basil leaves.
- Serve warm on lamb or beef.

Char-grilled Fillet Steak with Chilli Lime Salsa Verde

Serves 4

This is a typical Australian recipe which uses good steak, preferably fillet steak, that is grilled and then sauced. Have fun as the sauces may be interchanged and can be duplicated or tripled for more guests.

INGREDIENTS

Kitchen string	1.5 m
Fillet steaks	4, each 100–120 g, about 2.5-cm thick
Olive oil or cooking oil	1 Tbsp
Freshly ground black pepper	2 tsp
Salt	1 tsp

METHOD

- Tie a piece of string around the middle of each steak to ensure a neat shape and even cooking.
- Rub steaks with oil and pepper.
- See pg 79 for barbecue timings.
- Sprinkle with salt and leave to rest for 5 minutes.
- Cut string and remove. Serve warm, topped with chilli lime salsa verde*.

Note: Use tender cuts such as fillet steak for this dish.

*Chilli Lime Salsa Verde

INGREDIENTS

Lime juice	2 Tbsp
Cooking oil	1 Tbsp
Garlic	2 cloves, peeled and chopped
Chilli paste	2 tsp

METHOD

- Mix all the ingredients together to make salsa verde.

Char-grilled Point or Eye Fillet with Garlic Sauce

Serves 4

> The fillet steak is wrapped before cooking to keep its shape while cooking. Any good steak or lamb chops can be enjoyed with the prepared sauce. Serve warm.

INGREDIENTS

Garlic aioli sauce with coriander (see pg 45)	1 recipe
Kitchen string	for tying
Fillet steaks	4, each 100–120 g, about 2.5-cm thick
Olive oil or cooking oil	1 Tbsp
Garlic	2 cloves, peeled and pounded well
Freshly ground black pepper	2 tsp
Salt	to taste or $1/2$ tsp per steak

METHOD

- Prepare garlic sauce beforehand and keep warm.
- Tie a piece of string around the middle of each steak to ensure a neat shape and even cooking.
- Rub steaks with oil, garlic and pepper, keeping shape of steaks intact. Use the back of the cleaver to pound meat to break some of the fibres.
- See pg 79 for barbecue timings.
- After steaks are cooked, sprinkle with salt and leave to rest for 5 minutes.
- Cut string and remove.
- Serve warm, topped with some warmed garlic sauce, with some vegetables and crusty bread or *roti* on the side.

Note: Besides fillet steak, you can also use other tender cuts such as point of fillet.

Assorted Vegetables BBQ Platter

> When preparing capsicums, remember that each capsicum has a thin outer skin that peels off and it can be removed when the capsicum is roasted or grilled. The juicy underlayer is soft and moist and is used for salads and toppings.

INGREDIENTS

Chinese broccoli (*Kai lan*) stems	5, with some leaves left on
Banana leaves	2 pieces
Olive oil or butter	4 Tbsp

METHOD

- Shave off thick skin at base of stems. Wash and trim ends by slicing them off and cut into 80 g pieces.
- Cook on banana leaves, brushing with olive oil or butter, until medium soft, for about 20 minutes.

INGREDIENTS

Mushrooms	150 g
Asparagus spears	150 g
Chinese broccoli (*Kai lan*) stems	5
Tomatoes	3, firm and ripe
Banana leaves	3–4 pieces

METHOD

- Treat vegetables the same way as capsicums. Place them on buttered or oiled banana leaf on grill plate and cook for about 20 minutes.

INGREDIENTS

| Asparagus spears | 6, 40 g each |
| Banana leaves | 3–4 pieces |

METHOD

- Wash and trim ends by slicing them off.
- Cook on buttered banana leaf on medium heat until soft, for about 10 minutes.

INGREDIENTS

Whole red capsicum (bell peppers)	1, 150–180 g
Whole green capsicum (bell peppers)	1, 150–180 g
Olive oil or vegetable oil	1 Tbsp
Freshly ground black pepper	to taste

METHOD

- Grill on very high heat on a BBQ, at about 160°C. If using the grill plate, cook for 20 minutes.
- Coat capsicums with olive oil or vegetable oil and pepper.
- Cook until blackened. Cool and peel away crisp skin.
- Serve capsicum flesh as part of the vegetable platter or as part of meat or fish platter.

INGREDIENTS

Field mushrooms	50 g pieces
Grated ginger	2 tsp
Grated garlic	2 tsp
Grated lemon grass	2 tsp
Olive oil or vegetable oil	125 ml
Freshly ground black pepper	to taste

METHOD

- Wipe mushrooms with a clean towel but do not wash.
- Top with grated ginger, garlic, lemon grass, oil and pepper.
- Barbecue for 20 minutes.
- Add salt and pepper to serve.

INGREDIENTS

Ordinary tomatoes or Egg (Roma) tomatoes	3–4, 80 g each
Olive oil	85 ml
Freshly ground black pepper	to taste

METHOD

- Cook on buttered banana leaf with oil and pepper until tomatoes are soft, caramelised and juicy.
- Serve on vegetable platter. You may also use grilled onion or sweet corn.

Note: Serve Assorted Vegetables BBQ Platter with any of the sauces found on pg 74.

Char-grilled Steak with Coconut Lemon Grass Chilli Jam Sauce

Serves 4

▌ This recipe can be used with any tender and moist cut of meat.

INGREDIENTS

Coconut lemon grass
  chilli jam sauce* or
  Tamarind steak sauce
  (see pg 57)   1 recipe
T-bone steak, fillet steak
  or lamb from rump
  or leg   4, each 125 g, 2-cm
                       thick
Olive oil   1 Tbsp
Freshly ground
  black pepper   1 tsp
Salt   to taste

METHOD

- Prepare sauce beforehand.
- Slice steaks from the most tender cut of meats.
- Using the back of your knife, pound meat to break some of the fibres, taking care to keep meat in their original shapes.
- Drizzle steaks with oil. Sprinkle with pepper and add 2 Tbsp sauce on meat as it cooks.
- For outdoor BBQ, grill over hot coals or BBQ plate. For indoor grill, preheat ridged cast-iron grill over high heat.
- See pg 79 for barbecue timings.
- Sprinkle with salt. Leave to rest for 5 minutes.
- Serve warm with more warmed sauce and a serving of grilled vegetables.

*Coconut Lemon Grass Chilli Jam Sauce

Yields 700 ml

This sauce is best used for prawns as the combination is simple yet flavoursome and delicate enough for the simplicity of prawns. This is a spicy sauce and should be served chilled.

INGREDIENTS

Vegetable oil or olive oil 30 ml
Red chillies   100 g, seeded and
                            diced
Green chillies   1/2, seeded and diced
Lemon grass (serai)   1/2 stalk, diced
Garlic   2 cloves, peeled and
                            diced
Tomato   1, peeled, seeded and
                            diced
Coconut milk   500 ml
Ground coriander   2 tsp
Prawn (shrimp) paste
  (sambal belacan)   2 tsp
Palm sugar
  (gula Melaka)   2 tsp

METHOD

- Heat oil in a pan and sauté chillies, lemon grass, garlic and tomatoes until golden brown.
- Add coconut milk, coriander, prawn paste and sugar. Boil for 8–10 minutes. Stir slowly until sauce has thickened slightly.
- Remove from heat and pour into a blender. Purée until smooth, then chill and serve with grilled prawns or lobster.
- This can be made beforehand and kept aside until necessary.

Char-grilled Sirloin Steak with Coconut Lemon Grass Chilli Jam

Serves 4

A simple steak, brushed with oil and pre-prepared sauce.

INGREDIENTS

Coconut lemon grass chilli jam sauce (see pg 12)	4 x 700 ml
Sirloin steak, eye of rump or BBQ steak	4, each 250 g, 2.5-cm thick
Light olive oil	1 Tbsp
Freshly ground black pepper	1 tsp
Salt	to taste

METHOD

- Make chilli jam sauce beforehand.
- Brush steaks with olive oil and 2 Tbsp chilli jam sauce.
- Sprinkle with pepper.
- See pg 79 for barbecue timings.
- Sprinkle with salt and leave to rest for 5 minutes.
- Serve warm, topped with more warmed chilli jam sauce.

Spiced Beef Skewers with Sour Cream

Serves 4

A simple recipe mixed together and wrapped in a banana leaf.

INGREDIENTS

Onion	1, peeled and finely chopped
Garlic	4 cloves, peeled and diced
Chuck steak or beef	500 g, minced
Curry powder	1 Tbsp
Ginger	2.5-cm knob, peeled and ground
Star anise	2 tsp, pounded
Lemon pepper	2 tsp
Kaffir lime leaves	2
Salt	2 tsp
Sour cream	150 ml
Salt and black pepper	to taste
Banana leaf	1, cut into 8 squares, 20 x 20-cm each
Wooden skewers	8

METHOD

- In a frying pan (skillet), fry onion and garlic in some oil until aromatic.
- Place minced steak, spices with half the sour cream, salt and pepper in a food processor; pulse until combined. Add in more sour cream as needed and combine. Divide into 8 equal-sized portions.
- With wet hands, make sausage-like portions and place in the centre of an oiled banana leaf. Roll into cigar-like shapes and secure leaf with a skewer.
- For outdoor grill, grill over medium-hot coals.
  For indoor grill, preheat overhead grill.
- When grilling banana leaf sausages, keep brushing with oil so that they stay moist and do not burn. Grill sausages, turning every 2 minutes, until well browned but still juicy and slightly pink inside, for 8–10 minutes.

Note: Prepare meat up to 1 day in advance. Cover with cling film and refrigerate.

Moulded Beef Satay on Lemon Grass with Honey Tamarind Glaze

Serves 4

This is a simple recipe that involves moulding and wrapping meat around lemon grass stems for grilling. Serve these satays with char-grilled onions.

INGREDIENTS

Chuck steak	800 g, minced
Ginger	2.5-cm knob, peeled and grated
Galangal (*lengkuas*)	1/2 Tbsp, thinly sliced for grinding
Lemon grass (*serai*)	4 stalks, thinly sliced for grinding + 8 stalks, each 15-cm long
Garlic	2 cloves
Coriander (cilantro) leaves	55 g
Coriander (cilantro) root	1
Turmeric	1/2 tsp, ground
Chilli paste	2 tsp
Cumin	1 tsp, roasted and ground
Cardamon pods	1/2 tsp, ground
Salt	2 tsp
Freshly ground black pepper	1/2 tsp

GLAZE

Tamarind purée or paste	1 1/2 Tbsp
Honey	1 1/2 Tbsp
Salt and black pepper	to taste
Chilli	to taste

METHOD

- Place all ingredients except lemon grass stems and glaze ingredients in a food processor. Keep pulsing to mix well, until combined.
- Divide into 8 equal-sized portions.
- With wet hands, mould each portion around each lemon grass stem, into the shape of a sausage about 10-cm long.
- To make glaze, combine glaze ingredients. Increase the amount of chilli for taste, but not by too much or else balance will be lost.
- For outdoor BBQ, grill over medium-hot coal. For indoor grill, preheat overhead grill.
- Brush with glaze, turning every 2 minutes until well browned, but still juicy and slightly pink inside, for 8–10 minutes.

Note: Dark, shiny tamarind purée, sometimes referred to as concentrated purée or paste, is usually available from Asian or Indian grocery stores. If you can't find it, dissolve 2 Tbsp tamarind pulp in 2 Tbsp boiling water, then cool and press through a sieve for a concentrate.

Char-grilled Onions

In Asia, onions are cooked and served in more ways than anywhere else in the world. We fry them, grind them and cook them into *sambals*. We even steam and stir-fry onions and here I am attempting to barbecue them. They may be served on their own or with a large platter of meat.

INGREDIENTS

Brown or red onions	about 200 g each, large, unpeeled and cut into halves
Vinegar	2 Tbsp
Olive oil	2 Tbsp
Salt and black pepper	to taste
Mint leaves	1 sprig, finely chopped

METHOD

- Trim and peel each onion half and skewer them across so that they stay intact when cooking.
- Arrange onion halves, cut side up, on an oven tray. Sprinkle evenly with vinegar, oil, salt, pepper and mint.
- For outdoor BBQ, use grill or BBQ plate.
- Grill over medium-hot coals until lightly charred, for 7–8 minutes per side.
- For indoor grill, preheat overhead grill.
- Grill until lightly charred, for 5 minutes per side or until the onions are aromatic and look charred.

Tenderloin with Onions
(may be converted to Noodle dish)

Serves 4

This is another simple recipe that uses ingredients familiar to us in Asia. The meat may be used in a noodle dish after it is grilled.

INGREDIENTS
Marinade

Lime juice	2 Tbsp
Light soy sauce	2 Tbsp
Cooking oil	2 Tbsp
Coconut lemon grass chilli jam sauce (see pg 12)	2 Tbsp
Ginger	5-cm knob, peeled and grated
Coriander (cilantro) leaves or Vietnamese mint leaves (*daun kesum*)	¹/₂ bunch, pounded into paste
Leeks	8, sliced lengthwise and trimmed to 20-cm
Cumin	1 Tbsp, dry-roasted and roughly pounded
Coarse salt	1¹/₂ tsp
Beef tenderloin steaks	500–750 g, cut into 2.5-cm thick pieces
Toasted sesame oil	2 tsp
Lime	¹/₂, juiced
Coriander (cilantro) leaves	55 g, very finely pounded

METHOD
- Mix marinade ingredients together and marinate meat for 20 minutes.
- Mix cumin with salt.
- Rub steaks on both sides with sesame oil, then coat with spice mixture.
- Preheat grill. Place steaks on grill with marinade, cover and cook until done.
- Garnish with cumin and coriander leaves. Serve by cutting steaks into 2-cm slices. Serve while hot.

Note: The dish can be easily converted into a noodle stir-fry. Simply toss some pre-softened egg noodles or rice noodles on the grill so that there will be extra flavour with the leek and the juices. Then top with sliced beef. Note that the noodles will turn dark from all the grilling but this is part of the excitement of cooking on a BBQ plate.

Thai Beef Salad with Vietnamese Mint (*Daun Kesum*)

Serves 4

This is a dish made from meat that has been grilled briefly and then tossed into a salad with the most delectable of ingredients like Vietnamese mint and garlic. It is best served with warm freshly grilled meat and cold vegetables.

INGREDIENTS

Garlic	2 cloves, peeled
Vietnamese mint (*daun kesum*)	55 g, chopped
Mint leaves	55 g, torn
Sugar	1 1/2 tsp
Freshly ground black pepper	1 tsp
Light soy sauce	2 Tbsp
Thai fish sauce	2 Tbsp
Olive oil or vegetable oil	1 Tbsp
Boneless rump or sirloin steak	500 g, thinly scored across the grain

Dressing

Garlic and minced	4 cloves, peeled
Red or green chillies	4, seeded and thinly diced
Palm sugar (*gula Melaka*)	2 Tbsp, mixed with 3 Tbsp water and melted over heat
Thai fish sauce	60 ml
Lime juice	85 ml
Lime	1, rind grated

Salad

Lettuce leaves	6, large, torn into pieces
Green mangoes	2, small and firm, sliced thinly with skin left on
Cucumber	1, small, seeded and sliced into thin slivers
Green and unripe papaya (paw paw)	100 g, peeled then thinly sliced lengthwise
Water convolvulus (*kang kong*)	10 stems, hollow stems sliced lengthwise and left uncooked

Garnish

Vietnamese mint (*daun kesum*)	125 g, left whole for garnishing

METHOD

- Use a mortar and pestle to combine garlic, Vietnamese mint, mint, sugar and pepper. Mash to a paste. Stir in soy sauce, fish sauce and oil.
- Rub mixture all over steak. Marinate for 1 hour at room temperature or refrigerate covered for up to 4 hours.
- Preheat grill. Cook beef on high heat for about 5 minutes for rarely done and 8–10 minutes for medium rare. Turn it once, midway through the cooking time. Set aside to cool.
- To make dressing, use a mortar and pestle to combine garlic and chillies. Mash to a paste. Stir in sugar, fish sauce and lime juice. Set aside.
- Toss salad ingredients together with 2 1/2 Tbsp of dressing.
- Thinly slice beef across the grain. Toss with remaining salad.
- Divide salad between 4 plates and carefully serve with a slice of beef on top, with Vietnamese mint leaves as garnish.

Note: It is simple to put this dish together. The recipe will work with barbecued pork, lamb or chicken. The beef and vegetables can be prepared beforehand and refrigerated. Toss with sufficient dressing to suit your taste.

Butterflied Leg of Lamb *Panggang* with Green Mint Salsa

Serves 4–6

A grilled leg of lamb is best done over a spit, but you can also barbecue a piece of meat by turning over the piece as soon as one side is done. Here the leg was deboned and butterflied then coated with paste and tied into a roll. When grilled on the BBQ, the flavours are light and tasty.

INGREDIENTS

Leg of lamb	2 kg, butterflied (see pg 79)
Green mint salsa*	1 recipe
Flat metal skewers	2, each 34-cm long

Panggang paste

Red onions	2, peeled and chopped
Garlic	6 cloves, peeled
Coriander (cilantro) leaves	1 handful
Ginger	4-cm knob, peeled and chopped
Lime juice	1 Tbsp
Chillies	6, seeded
Tomato sauce	1 Tbsp
Almond meal	3 Tbsp, from 75 g dry-roasted almonds
Balsamic vinegar	2 Tbsp
Salt and black pepper	to taste

METHOD

- Place paste ingredients in a food processor; pulse to a smooth paste. Balance with salt and pepper. You may also be able to use about half the quantity of paste with any other lamb cutlets or chops in the same way except that the cooking time will be considerably shortened to about 15–20 minutes for 600–700 g of lamb chops or trimmed meat (fat removed).
- Butterfly meat.
- Open out flap and spread meat flat out like a book. Make another horizontal cut in the thick meat opposite and open out flat to form a butterfly shape.
- Push paste deep into slits. Insert skewers diagonally from opposite corners through butterflied lamb to hold it flat and keep paste in place. It will also be easier to hold and to turn lamb with skewers.
- For outdoor BBQ, grill over medium-hot coals, turning once.
- For indoor grill, preheat overhead grill. Arrange lamb on a wire rack over an oven tray.
- Grill, turning once, for 15 minutes per side for medium-rare and 20–25 minutes per side for well-done.
- As the lamb is grilling, add more paste and some oil on both sides.
- Remove to a board, cover with foil and leave to rest for 10 minutes, before slicing.
- Sprinkle with salt and pepper. Serve warm with green mint salsa (optional).

*Green Mint Salsa

Yields 175 ml

Green mint salsa goes very well with lamb, fish and vegetables. While ordinary mint is commonly used for sauces, the use of Vietnamese mint (*daun kesum*) has the punch of coriander mingled with the flavour of mint and makes an interesting combination.

INGREDIENTS

Vietnamese mint (*daun kesum*)	100 g
Mint leaves	3 springs
Garlic	1 clove, peeled and crushed
Mustard	1 tsp
Spring onions (scallions)	4
Semi-ripe mangoes	2, flesh chopped
Red wine vinegar or Chinese vinegar	1 Tbsp
Olive oil	125 ml
Sugar	to taste
Salt and black pepper	to taste

METHOD

- Place herbs, garlic, mustard, spring onions, mangoes, vinegar and oil in a food processor; blend to purée. Add sugar.
- Add salt and pepper to taste. Cover and let stand for 30 minutes at room temperature for flavours to blend. Serve at room temperature.
- This salsa can be made 3 days in advance. Refrigerate covered. Bring to room temperature and stir before serving.

Eurasian *Limau* Lamb Chops with Sour Sweet *Pesmol* Sauce

Serves 4

Chops are the simplest of cuts that cook evenly with a bit of fat around the edges, giving moisture and flavour.

INGREDIENTS

Lamb loin chops	8 cutlets, about 60 g each
Chilli paste	1 Tbsp
Metal skewers	8
Sour sweet *pesmol* sauce*	1 recipe

METHOD

- Trim off excess fat from cutlets. Cut around bone to release meat.
- Rub chilli paste on chops.
- Use half of the *pesmol* sauce on chops, grill and then keep chops warm until ready to serve.
- For outdoor BBQ, grill over hot coals. For indoor grill, preheat a ridged cast-iron grill pan over high heat.
- Grill for 3 minutes per side for medium-rare and 5 minutes per side for well-done.

Note: If there is enough time for early preparation, skewer and rub lamb with chilli up to 1 day in advance. Cover tightly with cling film and refrigerate. Make dressing up to 4 hours in advance. Cover and store at room temperature. Instead of metal skewers, you can also use bamboo or satay skewers.

*Sour Sweet *Pesmol* Sauce

Yields 500 ml

A sweet sour Javanese sauce made from coconut milk, turmeric and a sour element. Here I use rice wine for sourness.

INGREDIENTS

Vegetable oil or olive oil	1 Tbsp
Shallots	2, peeled and chopped
Garlic	2 cloves, peeled and chopped
Tomato paste	1 Tbsp
Red chillies	4, seeded and chopped
Ginger	3-cm knob, peeled and chopped
Greater galangal	3-cm knob, peeled and chopped
Lemon grass (*serai*)	1 stalk, crushed
Ground turmeric	$1/2$ tsp
Coconut milk	500 ml
Sugar	to taste
Shao Hsing wine	1 Tbsp

METHOD

- Heat oil in a saucepan and sauté all ingredients, except for ground turmeric, coconut milk, sugar and wine, for 3–5 minutes until light brown.
- Sprinkle in ground turmeric and continue to sauté for another 2 minutes.
- Slowly stir in coconut milk and sugar. Bring to the boil and let it simmer for about 8 minutes until sauce begins to thicken. Stir occasionally.
- Add wine and simmer for another 3 minutes.
- Remove saucepan from heat. Put sauce in a blender and process until smooth. Remove and keep warm.

Garlic Lamb Slices Grilled with Curry Leaves and Mint Sauce

Serves 4

▌ This is another simple recipe made elaborate with sauces.

INGREDIENTS

Lamb from neck rack or lamb loin chops	480 g, thinly sliced
Curry leaves and mint sauce* or sour sweet *pesmol* sauce (see pg 23)	1 recipe
Garnish	
Curry leaves	

METHOD

- Trim off excess fat from cutlets. Cut around bone to release meat.
- Brush half of the sauce on lamb pieces and grill slowly on BBQ or hot coals for about 15 minutes but do not burn paste.
- For outdoor BBQ, grill over hot coals. For indoor grill, preheat a ridged cast-iron grill pan over high heat.
- Grill for 3 minutes per side for medium-rare and 5 minutes per side for well-done.
- Drizzle the rest of the sauce over lamb and serve with rice or *roti*. Garnish with some fresh curry leaves.

Note: If there is enough time for early preparation, you can skewer and rub lamb with 2 tsp tamarind purée up to 1 day in advance. Cover tightly with cling film and refrigerate. Make sauce up to 4 hours in advance. Cover and store at room temperature.

*Curry Leaves and Mint Sauce

Yields about 650 ml

This is a pleasantly mild curry leaves sauce cooked exactly like a basil pesto, which is an Italian sauce normally served with pasta and cheese. To showcase our local flavours, I have used curry leaves here with great success.

INGREDIENTS

Olive oil or blended vegetable oil	1 Tbsp
Shallots	30 g, peeled and finely diced
Garlic	3 cloves, peeled and finely diced
Galangal (*lengkuas*)	2.5-cm knob, peeled and finely sliced
Ginger	2.5-cm knob, peeled and finely sliced
Lemon grass (*serai*)	1 stalk, crushed
Curry leaves	100 g, dry-roasted for 10 minutes in a dry wok
Prawn (shrimp) paste (*sambal belacan*)	1 Tbsp, dry-roasted
Tamarind purée	1 Tbsp or to taste
Green chillies	200 g or 10, seed half and dice all
Coconut milk	200 ml

METHOD

- Heat oil in a saucepan. Sauté shallots, garlic, galangal, ginger, lemon grass and curry leaves until light brown.
- Add shrimp paste, tamarind purée and green chillies and sauté for another 2–3 minutes.
- Pour in coconut milk and bring to the boil. Simmer for about 5 minutes, stirring gently until reduced to a thick sauce.
- Remove from heat and blend in a food processor. Blend for 2–4 minutes until smooth.
- Serve with meat or fish.

Goat Leg Tandoori on the Barbie

Serves 4–6, depending on amount of rice served on the side

INGREDIENTS

Whole goat or goat meat	2 kg, cut into pieces
Large metal skewer	1
Fat or clarified butter (ghee)	2 Tbsp
Limes	2, juiced
Rock salt	2 tsp, or to taste

Tandoori paste (or use a commercial tandoori paste)

Cloves	10
Coriander seeds	1 Tbsp, dry-roasted then ground
Cumin	1 Tbsp, dry-roasted then ground
Cardamom pods	8
Spanish onion	300 g, peeled and diced
Garlic	4 cloves, dry-roasted in coals
Ginger	4-cm knob, peeled and diced
Chilli powder	2 tsp, or to taste
Freshly ground black pepper	1 tsp
Saffron threads	$1/2$ tsp, soaked in 1 Tbsp warm milk
Ground turmeric	$1/2$ tsp
Thick yoghurt	350 g
Red or orange food colouring	

Salad

Tomatoes	4, firm, quartered
Lime	$1/2$, juiced
Freshly ground black pepper	to taste
Star fruit (optional)	

METHOD

- Skewer goat so that the leg can be easily handled. Puncture meat and insert fat in the punctured holes and slits on the thigh.
- Prepare tandoori paste by dry-roasting spices for 30 seconds in the microwave or oven until aromatic. Blend well, making sure that all spices are blended before adding onions.
- Blend all ingredients with yoghurt, adding colouring to give a lovely shade of orange.
- Sprinkle lime juice and rock salt onto meat and then spread paste all over. Slowly rotate on the BBQ, reapplying paste when it falls off.
- This is not the normal way for a tandoor to work but a suitable effect can be achieved if meat is rotated slowly for about 1 hour or until cooked and crisping. The BBQ should be on low, regular heat.
- Carve meat off the BBQ and serve with a fresh tomato salad with cooked mushrooms and some ghee rice. A simple salad can be made up of some quartered tomatoes, fresh lime juice and lashings of freshly ground black pepper. You can also use green tomatoes. For contrasting colour, add some star fruit.

Note: As goat does not have fat, the addition of ghee before grilling is a good idea. Any of the sauces in this book will go well with goat, however the curry leaves and mint sauce (see pg 24) will be best, when served on carved meat and ghee rice. This is a Western recipe with Eastern adaptations, so serve it as you like.

Lamb with Plum and *Hoisin* Glaze

Serves 6

INGREDIENTS

Plum sauce	120 ml
Hoisin sauce	30 g
Chilli paste	30 g
Garlic	3 cloves, peeled and blended
Shao Hsing wine	1 Tbsp
Lamb chops or cutlets	800 g, about 6 chops, trimmed of fat
Potatoes	3, boiled, thickly sliced and buttered with 2 Tbsp melted butter or olive oil
Salt and black pepper	to taste

METHOD

- Combine sauces, chilli paste, garlic and wine. Add lamb to mixture and mix well. Refrigerate for 2–3 hours or overnight.
- Cook lamb on heated BBQ for about 15 minutes until grilled and aromatic.
- Serve on a bed of buttered potatoes sprinkled with some salt and pepper.

Char-roasted Aubergine (Eggplant) with *Taucheo* Sesame and Honey *Miso* Glaze

Serves 4, when served with a meal

A different method with a similar theme. You should only try this in the BBQ for effect.

INGREDIENTS

Honey *miso* sauce or plain *miso* mixed with honey	4 Tbsp + extra for drizzling
Black bean paste (*taucheo*)	2 Tbsp
Sesame seeds	1 Tbsp
Aubergines (eggplants)	8, each 100 g

METHOD

- To make glaze, combine honey *miso* sauce, black bean paste and sesame seeds.
- Prick aubergines all over with a fork. Cut aubergines lengthwise and score a criss-cross pattern 1-cm deep in the flesh. Brush scored side with glaze.
- Grill glazed side down until sizzling and tender, then turn and grill for a further 5 minutes.
- Serve warm with extra honey *miso* sauce.
- For outdoor BBQ, grill over medium coals. For indoor grill, preheat overhead grill.

- Grill and turn frequently until charred all over, for 15 minutes.
- Leave to cool until cool enough to handle, for about 10 minutes.
- Prepare for serving as before.

Note: This goes well with any of the grilled or barbecued seafood dishes. You can grill aubergines first while seafood is cooking.

 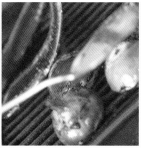 

Spiced Lamb Ribs with *Charmoula* Marinade

Serves 4–6

The lamb pieces are best seasoned with *Charmoula* or Middle Eastern/Moroccan marinade and then grilled or baked.

INGREDIENTS

Lamb ribs	500 g
Charmoula marinade*	2 recipes
Salt and black pepper	to taste

METHOD

- Slice carefully through each rib bone, trimming fat but keeping meat intact. Season using marinade and allow to sit for 2 hours.
- Barbecue on hot grill, turning often.
- For outdoor BBQ, grill over medium-hot coals. For indoor grill, preheat overhead grill.
- Grill, turning often, until well browned but still juicy and slightly pink inside for 8–10 minutes. Brush with marinade when grilling.
- Keep aside some marinade, add 1 Tbsp water and mix well to make sauce.
- Sprinkle meat with salt and pepper. Serve hot with sauce.

Charmoula Marinade

Yields 150 ml

INGREDIENTS

Coriander (cilantro) leaves	55 g
Coriander seeds	1/2 tsp, dry-roasted then ground
Garlic	6 cloves, peeled and crushed
Cumin	1 tsp, dry-roasted then ground
Chilli paste	2 tsp
Lime juice	2 Tbsp
Olive oil	2 Tbsp
Salt	to taste

METHOD

- Place all ingredients in a food processor; pulse to a paste. Use 1 recipe for 4 ribs.
- Prepare marinade 1 day in advance and marinate meat for better results.

Spiced Mutton Satay with Peanut Sauce on Polenta

Serves 4–6, with a meal

Satay, originally from Malaysia and Indonesia, is now enjoyed all over the world although we still have the best satay seasoning and sauce that can be used in countless ways. Traditional satay is lovely and tasty but preparing it can be time consuming. So here is an easy adaptation of the traditional satay. It is delicious when served with polenta.

INGREDIENTS

Topside lamb	500 g, deboned
Garlic	3 cloves, peeled, crushed and pounded
Ginger	2.5-cm knob, grated
Lemon grass (serai)	1 stalk, pounded with garlic paste
Olive oil	1 Tbsp
Coconut milk	3 Tbsp
Red chillies	2, seeded and pounded
Coriander seeds	1 tsp, ground
Tamarind paste or lime juice	1 Tbsp
Light soy sauce	1 Tbsp
Palm sugar (gula Melaka)	1 Tbsp
Salt	2 tsp
Freshly ground black pepper	1 tsp
Satay peanut sauce*	1 recipe (optional)
Wooden skewers	

METHOD

- Slice lamb across the grain into strips, about 15 x 2-cm wide, for threading onto skewers.
- Rub garlic, ginger and lemon grass into meat with a little oil and 1 tsp of coconut milk. Refrigerate covered for a few hours.
- Skewer lamb strips. Refrigerate covered.
- Place chillies, coriander, tamarind paste, coconut milk, soy sauce and palm sugar in a food processor; pulse to a paste.
- Spread paste evenly over skewered meat and refrigerate for 2 hours, spreading more paste if necessary.
- For outdoor BBQ, grill over medium-hot coals. For indoor grill, preheat overhead grill.
- Grill, turning every 2 minutes, until well browned but still juicy and slightly pink inside, for 8–10 minutes. Baste satay with more coconut milk.
- Sprinkle with salt and pepper. Serve mutton satay on polenta squares# with hot sauce or sticky rice.

Note: As a variation to this recipe, you may use sour sweet *pesmol* sauce (see pg 23) or coconut lemon grass chilli jam sauce (see pg 12).

*Satay Peanut Sauce

Yields 375 ml

This is a sauce that has lunched a million tourists. While you should really use dry-roasted peanuts to make an authentic peanut sauce, you can also make it successfully with peanut butter.

INGREDIENTS

Garlic	3 cloves, peeled
Spanish onions	2, medium, peeled and roughly chopped
Candlenuts or macadamia nuts	8
Lemon grass (serai) (white part only)	2 stalks, chopped
Cooking oil	1 Tbsp
Mixed Malaysian curry powder	1 1/2 Tbsp
Tamarind purée	1 1/2 Tbsp
Sambal oelek	2 Tbsp, or to taste
Unsalted, dry-roasted peanuts (groundnuts)	150 g, roughly ground or 125 ml crunchy peanut butter
Coconut milk	375 ml
Hot water	250 ml
Sugar and salt	to taste

METHOD

- Blend garlic, onions, candlenuts and lemon grass together until smooth.
- Heat oil on medium to high heat in a saucepan and sauté paste until caramelised, this will take at least 3–5 minutes. Stir constantly and add a little extra oil if necessary so that mixture does not stick to the bottom of the saucepan.
- Add curry powder, tamarind purée and *sambal oelek* to mixture and stir well. Fry on medium heat for a few minutes, add peanuts, coconut milk and hot water.
- Simmer until sauce is spreadable and can be poured easily. The sauce will reduce very quickly so it will need to be stirred continuously. If sauce is too thick, add some hot water and stir well. Add sugar and salt to taste.
- For those who like spicy peanut sauce, just add extra *sambal oelek*.

Note: If you grind the peanuts, make sure that they are roughly ground so that large crunchy pieces remain.

#Polenta

Serves 4–6

This is another version of semolina and can be made very quickly.

INGREDIENTS

Water	1.75 litres
Chicken stock	1 litre
Polenta (cornmeal)	500 g
Butter	50 g or 20 ml olive oil
Salt and black pepper	to taste

METHOD

- Combine water and stock in a heavy-based pan and bring to the boil on high heat. Gradually add polenta in a slow and steady stream, stirring constantly with a wooden spoon.
- Reduce to low heat and cook uncovered, stirring often for 30–35 minutes until thick, creamy and pale yellow.
- Stir in butter until well combined. Season with salt and pepper.
- Pour into a buttered pan with raised sides and spread it flat so that squares may be cut from the cooled polenta once it solidifies.
- Serve grilled satay on a 5 x 5-cm square of polenta. Serve with sauce of your choice with diced cucumber and tomatoes on the side.

Moroccan Lamb Skewers with Cous Cous

Serves 4

Although the ingredients used in this Middle Eastern recipe are similar to our spices, they are used differently to create a very unique taste.

INGREDIENTS
Marinade

Onion	50 g, small, peeled and grated
Olive oil	200 ml
Freshly ground black pepper	1 tsp
Dried oregano	2 tsp
Ground cinnamon	1 tsp
Ground cumin	2 tsp
Chilli powder	a pinch
Boneless leg of lamb	500 g, trimmed and cut into 4-cm cubes
Freshly ground black pepper	2 tsp
Dried oregano	2 tsp
Metal skewers	3–4
Red onion	200 g, large, peeled and cut into 2.5-cm pieces
Cherry tomato	125 g, green or half ripe, skewered
Green capsicums (bell peppers)	10, sliced into 4-cm pieces
Olive oil	60 ml
Salt and black pepper	to taste

METHOD
- Combine all marinade ingredients and mix well. Add lamb cubes and turn to coat. Add pepper and oregano.
- Refrigerate covered for up to 6 hours. Turn and leave for another 4 hours.
- Preheat grill. Thread lamb cubes onto skewers. Leave a little space between the pieces for onions and tomatoes if you want to use them. Discard used marinade.
- Grill lamb skewers in batches, to the desired degree of doneness. For medium-rare, grill for 3–4 minutes.
- Transfer lamb skewers to the same platter as cous cous*.

Note: Lamb cut from the leg makes the most succulent skewers. If you like, serve skewers with chilli jam or garlic sauce.

*Cous Cous

Serves 4–6

This is a type of semolina made by Middle Easterners.

INGREDIENTS

Cous cous	250 g
Boiling chicken stock or boiling water	250 ml
Butter or olive oil	1 Tbsp
Ground cumin	$1/2$ tsp
Dried oregano	$1/2$ tsp
Olive oil	1 Tbsp
Chilli	to taste
Salt and black pepper	to taste

METHOD
- Pour cous cous into a pan and add boiling stock.
- Leave mixture for 5 minutes to swell then slowly warm up with butter. Stir for a few minutes until it fluffs up, then fluff with a fork and season with rest of ingredients.
- Serve with lamb skewers.

Tikka Style Barbecued Lamb Served with Barbecued Pineapple with Rum Glaze

Serves 4

This is an Indian-style BBQ served with a yoghurt. It is normally cooked on a small grill over hot coals or in a tandoor. Use the same recipe with or without the meat skewers. If skewers are unavailable, grill on a BBQ.

INGREDIENTS

Boneless lamb	500 g, cubed

Marinade

Ginger	2 Tbsp, peeled and grated
Garlic	4 cloves, peeled and crushed
Mint	1 sprig, chopped
Ground cumin	1 Tbsp
Dried mango powder (*amchur*)	1 Tbsp
Ground turmeric	1 tsp
Thick yoghurt	150 ml
Green chillies	20, chopped

Naan or other flat bread	4
Salt and black pepper	to taste
Cucumber yoghurt *raita** (optional)	1 recipe
Metal skewers	2, each 35-cm long

*Cucumber Yoghurt *Raita*

Plain yoghurt	250 ml
Red onion	1, peeled and diced
Cucumber	1, peeled and flesh removed from centre, then diced
Green mango	1, small, peeled and diced (optional)
Green chilli	1, sliced
Salt and black pepper	to taste

METHOD

- Combine lamb cubes with all marinade ingredients. Toss well to coat evenly.
- Refrigerate covered for 4 hours. Thread lamb cubes onto skewers.
- Using outdoor BBQ, grill over medium-hot coals, turning every 2 minutes, until well browned but still juicy and slightly pink inside for 8–10 minutes.
- Warm *naan*, by setting directly onto the grill, for 1 minute per side.
- Using indoor grill, preheat overhead grill. Grill, turning every 2 minutes, until well browned but still juicy and slightly pink inside for 8–10 minutes.
- Briefly warm *naan* under the grill for 30 seconds per side.
- To make cucumber yoghurt *raita* (optional), mix all ingredients together.
- Sprinkle lamb cubes with salt and pepper. Serve hot with warm *naan*, cucumber yoghurt *raita* and barbecued pineapple with rum glaze#.

Note: Lamb cubes may be marinated 1 day in advance. For better flavour, do this then refrigerate covered until needed.

#Barbecued Pineapple with Rum Glaze

Serves 4

The pineapple cooked on the BBQ is a contrast to the meat but it gives great aroma and wonderful flavour, especially when served with rum or sugar syrup.

INGREDIENTS

Pineapple	1, medium-sized, unpeeled and quartered
Dark rum or sugar syrup	2 Tbsp
Lime juice	1 Tbsp
Honey	2 Tbsp

METHOD

- Cut away the core from pineapple quarters.
- For glaze, combine rum, lime juice and honey and stir to dissolve.
- Grill according to instructions below.
- Serve warm and drizzle over with any remaining glaze. Great with fish or prawn dishes.
- For outdoor BBQ, grill over medium-low coals. For indoor grill, preheat overhead grill.
- Brush with glaze and grill until hot and lightly charred, for 5–10 minutes per side.

Barbecued Chinese Style Ribs

Serves 4

The meats used in the recipe are interchangeable so that people of all races and religions can enjoy.

INGREDIENTS

Sauce

Vegetable oil	2 Tbsp
Ginger	1 Tbsp, peeled and minced
Garlic	2 cloves, peeled and minced
Chinese five-spice powder	1 tsp
Light or dark brown sugar	8 Tbsp, packed
Thick dark soy sauce (*kecap manis*)	60 ml
Shao Hsing wine	2 Tbsp
Chilli paste	1 tsp
Salt and black pepper	to taste
Star anise	1, pounded
Country-style pork ribs	1.25 kg
Cucumber	1, sliced and soaked in 125 ml vinegar
Pineapple	1/4, cubed

METHOD

- To prepare sauce, heat oil on medium heat in a saucepan. Add ginger and garlic and cook for about 8 minutes, stirring often until aromatic.
- Add remaining sauce ingredients. Simmer and cook for about 15 minutes. Stir often, until reduced to half.
- Rub star anise into ribs. Preheat BBQ and oil grill plate.
- Season ribs with salt and pepper. Brush all over with barbecue sauce.
- Grill for about 5-6 minutes. Continue cooking until glaze is browned but not burned. Check ribs often, removing the ones that have browned, and continue cooking the rest.
- Serve with rice balls* and a side salad of cucumber and pineapple.

*RICE BALLS

- Cook rice as usual. While rice is still warm, add 2 Tbsp butter and mix.
- Use your hands to make rice balls. You may add chopped basil to rice before making rice balls.
- Leave to cool. Warm slightly in the microwave for 1 minute just before serving. Do not overcook or rice balls will break apart.

Chinese Vinegar Pork Chops

Serves 4

Pork chops are usually used in soy sauce dishes but the use of Chinese vinegar in this recipe helps to change the flavours for an interesting balance.

INGREDIENTS

Pork chops	100–120 g

Paste

Garlic	4 cloves, peeled and pounded
Black peppercorns	2 Tbsp
Star anise	1, pounded
Chilli paste	1 tsp
Thai sweet basil leaves (*kemangi*)	2 Tbsp
Black Chinese vinegar	2 Tbsp + extra for basting
Brown sugar	1 tsp
Olive oil	3 Tbsp

METHOD

- Trim off excess fat from chops. With scissors, cut snips through the remaining fat at 4-cm intervals so that the chops do not fold up. If the chops are too thick, they may be frenched or butterflied (see pg 79) and the paste stuffed into the space created.
- Place paste ingredients in a food processor; pulse to a coarse paste.
- Rub paste over both sides of chops. You can rub pork with paste up to 2 hours in advance.
- Refrigerate covered until ready to use.
- For outdoor BBQ, grill over medium-hot coals. For indoor grill, preheat a ridged cast-iron grill pan over high heat.
- Grill, basting with extra vinegar, until there is no trace of pink near the bone but pork is still juicy, for 8–10 minutes per side.

Note: These chops are delicious served with barbecued root vegetables*.

---

*Barbecued Root Vegetables

Here are some ways of preparing root vegetables for barbecuing or char-grilling.

Root vegetables	
Sweet potato, Potato, Butternut pumpkin	80 g pieces, skins left on
Carrot	70–80 g pieces, peeled

METHOD

- To BBQ, slow-cook in a closed BBQ at 160°C.
- Use a banana leaf on the BBQ plate, covering the vegetables with coriander (cilantro) or mint and some butter, olive or vegetable oil and shavings of palm sugar to glaze. Sprinkle with some salt.
- Barbecue for 40–60 minutes, until vegetables are soft, golden and caramelised. They should be sticky and very tender.
- Brush some oil on vegetables continuously while grilling.
- Instead of barbecuing, you can char-grill for 25–30 minutes on a grill pan. Brush with oil or butter when vegetables are being grilled.

Mexican Pork Strips Barbecued and Served with Pineapple Lime Salsa

Serves 4

Pork cooked with chilli and mint is a refreshing change, especially when served with a lime salsa that removes the fat from the flavour.

INGREDIENTS

Pork neck	500 g
Garlic	4 cloves, peeled and crushed
Freshly ground black pepper	1/2 tsp
Ground cumin	1 tsp
Golden syrup	1 Tbsp
Chilli powder	1 Tbsp
Mint	30 g, roughly chopped
Olive oil	2 Tbsp
Salt and black pepper	to taste
Dried lotus leaves or fresh turmeric	4 pieces, soaked in water to reconstitute leaves
Pineapple lime salsa*	1 recipe

METHOD

- Trim fat from pork neck and slice into 4 x 12-cm strips.
- Combine remaining ingredients except leaves and salsa.
- Rub mixture to coat thoroughly.
- Cover and refrigerate for 4 hours.
- Wrap meat in leaves and grill. To brown, remove leaves at the end.
- For outdoor BBQ, grill over medium-hot coals. For indoor grill, preheat a ridged cast-iron grill pan over high heat for about 20 minutes until plate is heated.
- Grill for 6–7 minutes until there is no trace of pink but make sure that pork is still juicy.
- Sprinkle with salt and pepper. Serve hot with pineapple lime salsa or serve cold as a salad.

*Pineapple Lime Salsa

Yields 375 ml

This may be used as a salad or as a dressing. It may be prepared and refrigerated up to 3–4 hours before use.

INGREDIENTS

Pineapple	500 g, cored and diced
Red chillies	3, seeded and chopped
Red onion	100 g, peeled and chopped
Coriander (cilantro) or mint leaves	3 Tbsp, chopped
Lime zest	grated from 1 lime
Lime juice	3 Tbsp
Salt	to taste
Chilli paste	1 Tbsp or to taste
Sugar	

METHOD

- Combine all ingredients.
- Cover and let stand for 30 minutes for flavours to blend. Serve chilled.

Pork Ribs in Sweet Sour Flavour

Serves 4

The ribs grill well on small BBQs or even under the oven grill in a small kitchen. Again, the ribs may be substituted by different meats, although using the same cuts is advisable.

INGREDIENTS

Pork spareribs	2 kg

Sweet sour mixture

Garlic	2 cloves, peeled and crushed
Ginger	2.5-cm knob, peeled and grated
Pineapple juice	125 ml
Thai fish sauce	2 Tbsp
Tomato purée	4 Tbsp
Lime juice	4 Tbsp
Golden syrup	2 Tbsp
Thai sweet chilli sauce	6 Tbsp

METHOD

- Separate ribs by slicing between bones.
- Cook for 2 minutes in boiling water.
- Prepare mixture. Stir-fry garlic and ginger until aromatic. Add rest of ingredients and simmer. Brush mixture on ribs.
- Sweet sour mixture can be prepared up to 1 day in advance. Refrigerate covered.
- For outdoor BBQ, grill very slowly over medium-hot coals. For indoor grill, preheat overhead grill.
- Grill, turning and basting frequently, until brown and crusty, for 15 minutes.

Spiced *Hoisin* Ribs

Serves 4

INGREDIENTS

Pork spareribs	2 kg
Hoisin sauce	8 Tbsp
Chinese five-spice powder	$1/2$ tsp
Garlic	4 cloves, peeled and crushed
Ginger	5-cm knob, peeled and grated
Medium dry sherry	2 Tbsp
Light soy sauce	4 Tbsp
Chinese vinegar	2 Tbsp, warmed
Dark brown sugar	8 Tbsp

METHOD

- Separate ribs by slicing between bones.
- Cook spareribs in boiling water for 2 minutes.
- Combine remaining ingredients and marinate ribs. Reserve 2 Tbsp for basting.
- Follow grilling instructions from previous recipe.

Spicy Pork Satay with Garlic Aioli Sauce with Coriander

Serves 4

Pork satay is popular with the Nyonyas in Malacca. For this dish, pork may be substituted with lamb or goat meat if required. The curry leaf sauce is particularly interesting with the satay.

INGREDIENTS

Pork neck	500 g

Paste

Star anise	2, pounded
Ground cinnamon	$1/2$ tsp
Ground turmeric	$1/2$ tsp
Paste from 2 stalks of lemon grass (*serai*)	2 Tbsp
Chilli paste	1 Tbsp
Light soy sauce	1 Tbsp
Sugar	1 tsp
Shao Hsing wine	3 Tbsp
Bamboo skewers	12, pre-soaked
Salt and black pepper	to taste
Garlic aioli sauce with coriander* or curry leaves and mint sauce (see pg 24)	1 recipe

METHOD

- Cut neck into small, thin slices that can be threaded onto a skewer.
- Place all the paste ingredients in a food processor; pulse to a smooth paste.
- Spread paste over both sides of the pork skewers.
- Refrigerate covered for 4 hours. The satay may be marinated 1 day in advance.
- Remove from refrigerator 1 hour just before grilling.
- For outdoor BBQ, grill over medium-hot coals. For indoor grill, preheat overhead grill.
- Grill until pork is opaque but still juicy, for about 3 minutes per side.
- Sprinkle with salt and pepper.
- Serve hot with garlic aioli sauce or curry leaves and mint sauce, brushing on liberally at the end.

Note: If heat is too intense, remove satay before it loses juicy flavours.

---

*Garlic Aioli Sauce with Coriander

Yields 125 ml

A garlic sauce similar to this is used in Asia for meat or fish, especially salmon.

INGREDIENTS

Garlic	2 bulbs, unpeeled
Olive oil	1 Tbsp
Salt and black pepper	to taste
Thai Sweet chilli sauce	2 tsp
Balsamic vinegar	2 Tbsp
Coconut milk or double cream	2 Tbsp
Coriander (cilantro) leaves	50 g
Thick yoghurt	150 ml
Salt and black pepper	to taste

METHOD

- Slice off the tops of garlic then place garlic cut-side up on the oven tray. Drizzle olive oil and sprinkle with salt and pepper. Roast for 1 hour until completely soft.
- Leave to cool until cool enough to handle. Squeeze out cloves of garlic from papery skins into a food processor.
- Add chilli sauce, vinegar, coconut milk, coriander and yoghurt; blend until smooth. Add salt and pepper to taste.
- Serve with lamb or beef. This sauce can be prepared up to 2 days in advance.

Note: Cloves may be roasted in the coals of an open fire.

Chicken Breasts Stuffed with Mint Pesto

Serves 4

This is a simple recipe with sophisticated flavour. A pesto is a sauce that may be spread or stuffed into pockets of meat for flavour. Mint is particularly tasty with chicken but the recipe may also be adapted for duck or turkey breasts.

INGREDIENTS

Pesto

Sundried tomatoes	5, packed in oil
Mint leaves	4 Tbsp, packed
Vietnamese mint leaves (*daun kesum*)	4 Tbsp, packed
Garlic	2 cloves, peeled and halved
Lemon zest	$1/2$ tsp, grated
Extra virgin olive oil	4 Tbsp
Salt	$1/2$ tsp or to taste
Freshly ground black pepper	$1/2$ tsp or to taste
Chicken breasts	2, about 500 g, deboned, skinned and cut into halves
Metal skewers	4
Olive oil	2 tsp
Salt and black pepper	to taste
Plain (all-purpose) flour	2 Tbsp, mixed with salt and black pepper

METHOD

- In a food processor, blend pesto ingredients. Process to a thick paste. Season with salt and pepper to taste.
- Flatten breasts and with a sharp knife, cut a slit about 4–5-cm down the rounded side of each breast.
- Open slit through chicken horizontally to create a pocket, taking care not to cut through the other side. Fill each pocket with one-quarter of the pesto. Skewer to hold pesto sauce in place.
- Brush olive oil on both sides of chicken and season with salt and pepper. Lightly dust plain flour onto chicken.
- Cook chicken, brushing with oil until cooked. Turn once midway through the cooking time.
- Serve on a bed of vegetables and pasta or noodles for a nice meal.

Chicken Mid-eastern

Serves 4–6

INGREDIENTS
Sauce
Chilli paste	1 Tbsp
Garlic	4 cloves, peeled and pounded
Sundried tomatoes	4, packed in oil
Lime rind	1 Tbsp, finely grated
Lime juice	125 ml
Chicken thighs	6

METHOD
- Prepare sauce by blending all sauce ingredients into a paste.
- Wash and dry chicken with kitchen paper. Place on cutting board and spread paste mixture onto chicken.
- Place on BBQ with oven tray underneath to collect juices.
- Turn chicken over often for 20 minutes until cooked.
- Serve with a green Middle Eastern salad called *Tabbouleh** and pieces of Lebanese bread or *roti*.

Tabbouleh

Serves 6

INGREDIENTS
Cracked wheat (*burgul*)	1 cup	
Broad-leaved parsley (Chinese coriander)	1 bunch, finely chopped	
Tomatoes	3, finely chopped	
Limes	2, juiced	
Vinegar	2 Tbsp, to taste	
Sugar	to taste	
Salt	to taste	
Chilli	to taste	
Freshly ground black pepper	to taste	

METHOD
- Soak wheat in warm water for 2 hours for it to expand. Drain water and dry fluff.
- Mix parsley leaves, tomatoes and wheat together.
- Mix all the juices and seasonings together, stirring sugar until blended.
- Pour over salad and toss well. Serve with chicken and bread.

Butterflied Chicken Tandoori

Serves 4

The tandoori was once only an Indian method of cooking but today it has spread all over the world. Here we use a small chicken so that it can be grilled on a BBQ by following the basic principles of the tandoor method.

INGREDIENTS

Chicken	about 1.5 kg
Metal skewers	2
Lime juice	1 Tbsp
Salt and black pepper	to taste

Tandoori mix

Cumin	2 tsp, dry-roasted
Ground coriander	2 tsp, dry-roasted
Garlic	6 cloves, peeled and blended
Ginger	2.5-cm knob, peeled
Chilli powder	1 tsp
Sweet paprika	1 tsp
Tomato paste	1 Tbsp
Red food colouring	a few drops
Lime	1, juiced
Vegetable or olive oil	1 Tbsp
Garlic	2 cloves, peeled and pounded
Green papaya (paw paw)	1, cut into thin slices, about 4-cm each
Yoghurt	60 ml

METHOD

- Place chicken on board. Using a sharp knife, cut backbone from the underneath side. Turn over and insert skewers to keep chicken flat.
- Coat whole chicken with lime juice, salt and pepper. Drain excess juice.
- Blend all tandoori mix ingredients together. Add garlic, papaya slices and yoghurt to tandoori mix then rub on chicken and coat evenly. Refrigerate covered for 1 hour.
- Barbecue or grill. Cover with wok lid for intense heat for about 45 minutes until chicken is cooked.
- Remove wok lid for browning effect.
- For outdoor BBQ, grill over medium-hot coals. For indoor grill, preheat overhead grill.
- Grill, turning every 3 minutes, until opaque with no trace of pink at the bone.
- Serve on a platter with rice, *roti* or *chappati*.
- Serve hot with mango pickle at the side.

Chicken Cacciatore Barbecued or Grilled with Garlic Bulbs

Serves 6

This is a classic Italian dish cooked in a simple tomato-based sauce. It is very tasty, especially when garlic is added whole. When the bulb becomes soft on the grill together with the chicken, it adds a rich flavour to this fast-cooking dish. For a different experience, use the BBQ as a cooking surface for the chicken and vegetables.

INGREDIENTS

Chicken	2 kg, cut into 4 large pieces, with skin left on
Garlic	2 bulbs, unpeeled but sliced across into two
Sweet potato	1, about 200 g, peeled and thickly sliced
Green capsicum (bell pepper)	1
Onion	1, peeled and ground into paste
Garlic	3 cloves, peeled and ground into paste
Olive oil	1 Tbsp
Canned chopped tomatoes	875 g
Balsamic vinegar	4 Tbsp
Sugar	1 tsp
Salt and black pepper	to taste

METHOD

- Flatten chicken so that it sits flat on grill.
- Brush oil on vegetables and grill slowly on BBQ or grill for 20–30 minutes, adding oil if necessary. Keep warm until needed.
- Brush onion and garlic on chicken and grill for 7 minutes, until cooked without getting charred. The vegetables are cooked when they are tender.
- Keep chicken warm until needed.
- Add tomatoes, vinegar and sugar to a saucepan and simmer. Add any extra garlic from grilled vegetables and cook to reduce.
- Season with salt and pepper. Spoon sauce over chicken, adding vegetables and serve. Add pasta to this for a nice meal.

Grilled Chicken Thighs or Breast Fillets for Caesar Salad

Serves 4

The Caesar Salad is well known in all its variations and is a special favourite of mine.

INGREDIENTS

Chicken breast fillets or thigh fillets	600–700 g
Olive oil	3 Tbsp
Limes	2, juiced
Egg	1, coddled (semi-cooked)

Garlic croutons

Butter	1 Tbsp
Bread	3 thin slices, trimmed of crust
Garlic	1 clove, peeled and blended into paste

Dressing

Extra virgin olive oil	3 Tbsp
Canned anchovy fillets	8, cut up
Worcestershire sauce	1 tsp
Dry mustard or prepared mustard	1 tsp
Mayonnaise	2 Tbsp
Salt	1 tsp
Freshly ground black pepper	1 1/2 tsp
Garlic	1 clove, peeled and blended into paste

Salad

Cos or Romaine lettuce (lettuce with long leaves or Chinese lettuce)	1, large
Lime	1
Parmesan cheese	25 g, freshly grated

METHOD

- If using thigh fillets, butterfly (see pg 79). Brush chicken with olive oil with lime juice. Marinate for 2 hours.
- Prepare salad. Make croutons by generously buttering bread and spreading garlic paste. Slice into cubes and toast until brown and crisp.
- To coddle egg, bring water to the boil in a pan. Place egg in water to cook for 1 minute. Remove pan from heat, leave egg in water to cook partially. Blanch egg in cold water. Use with salad. Egg will be half-cooked.
- Grill marinated chicken until browned. Slice thinly for salad.
- To make dressing, add oil to a bowl, then add rest of ingredients. Mix well.
- Assemble salad. Place lettuce at the bottom of the platter. Add rest of ingredients then toss well with dressing.
- Squeeze lime and add cheese and coddled egg. Top with a few croutons.

Crispy *Hoisin* Vinegar Duck

Serves 4

A *hoisin* duck recipe cooked on the BBQ is the simplest method of doing this dish, which works on the principle that the duck fat is slowly melted off, leaving the skin crisp. But you have to watch over the cooking carefully.

INGREDIENTS

Whole duck	1.5 kg or 6 duck breasts
Balsamic vinegar	6 Tbsp
Sweet chilli sauce	1 Tbsp
Hoisin sauce	2 Tbsp
Salt and black pepper	1 tsp each
Balsamic vinegar	1 Tbsp, extra for drizzling

Note: Marinate duck up to 2 hours in advance. Refrigerate covered. Serve with garlic aioli sauce (see pg 45) with a bit of orange juice added.

METHOD

- Score duck skin with a sharp knife by cutting shallow diagonal parallel slashes at 1-cm intervals to make diamond patterns. Be careful not to pierce the flesh. This scoring is important if you want a perfectly crisp duck. The scored surface allows the layer of fat under the skin to melt away so that the outer skin can crisp.
- Combine vinegar, chilli sauce and *hoisin* sauce in a shallow dish just wide enough to fit the duck. Add duck, skin side up. Cover and marinate for 20 minutes at room temperature.

Corn with Coriander Chilli Butter

Serves 4

Corn cooks well and is good for serving at an informal BBQ party where fingers and paper plates do just as well as anything else. Try this recipe for something different.

INGREDIENTS

Fresh sweetcorn	4 ears
Melted butter	2 Tbsp
Salt and black pepper	to taste
Coriander (cilantro)	
chilli butter*	4 slices, each
	1.5-cm thick
Lime	1, cut into wedges

METHOD

- Cut each ear of corn across into 2–3 pieces.
- Cook corn in boiling water for 2 minutes. Refresh in cold water. Brush with melted butter then grill or barbecue.
- For outdoor BBQ, grill over medium-hot coals. For indoor grill, preheat overhead grill.
- Grill, turning frequently until lightly charred, for 5 minutes, brushing frequently with oil or butter.
- Sprinkle with salt and pepper. Serve each piece warm with a slice of coriander chilli butter and a wedge of lime.

*Coriander Chilli Butter

Sufficient to cover 4 ears of corn

INGREDIENTS

Coriander (cilantro)	
leaves	50 g
Green chillies	2, seeded
Butter	3 Tbsp, melted
Salt	to taste

METHOD

- Blend coriander leaves and chillies in a mortar and pestle or food processor until well blended. Add butter and continue to blend, adding salt to taste.
- Shape mixture into small brick-shaped pieces. Freeze and use as required when corn is cooked.

Note: Coriander chilli butter can be prepared in advance and stored in the refrigerator.

- For outdoor grill or BBQ, grill over medium coals. Cook duck on low heat first for 5–8 minutes so that meat is cooked.
- Grill, with skin side down until skin is crispy, for 5 minutes. Turn and grill for a further 8 minutes for medium-rare and 10 minutes for well-done. Allow skin to crisp by oiling further and cooking skin side down, turning often to prevent burning.
- Cover with foil and leave to rest for 5 minutes before cutting into thin slices. Sprinkle with salt and pepper. Drizzle remaining balsamic vinegar over. Serve hot.

Minced Chicken Cooked as Egyptian Style Kebabs

Serves 4

> The dish is made with seasoned meat. First, the seasoning is added to the meat, then the meat is moulded and skewered. Finally, they are grilled and served with a plain salad or with any of the sauces in this book. As an alternative, you can use lemon grass stalks as skewers and make lemon grass kebabs.

INGREDIENTS

Marinade

Onion	1, 200 g, peeled and chopped
Garlic	4 cloves, peeled and chopped
Lemon juice	4 Tbsp
Fresh thyme or basil	1 Tbsp, chopped
Paprika	1 Tbsp
Cayenne pepper	$1/2$ tsp
Fresh basil	4 Tbsp, chopped
Freshly ground black pepper	$1/2$ tsp
Plain yoghurt	1 cup
Minced chicken	500 g
Wooden skewers	20, pre-soaked

METHOD

- Place all marinade ingredients in a food processor, except yoghurt; pulse until well combined.
- Add yoghurt and pulse until blended.
- Place blended marinade into a dish to mix with minced chicken.
- With oiled hands, form mixture into sausage-like pieces and thread onto skewers. You must press pieces firmly to hold. Refrigerate covered for 6–8 hours.
- Preheat grill and oil grill and kebabs. Grill kebabs until aromatic, turning once midway through the cooking time. Serve immediately.

Note: To accompany kebabs, grill skewers of capsicums (bell peppers) and mushrooms (see pg 10), brushed with some oil and then served with some *roti* or *chappati* and any of the sauces or a mixed dipping sauce of yoghurt, chopped onions and chilli.

Chinese Five-spice Quail or Chicken Pieces with Tamarind Steak Sauce

Serves 4

This is cooked with small quail, squab or chicken pieces and may be served cold or as soon as the birds are cooked. This is great picnic food as the birds are small and easy to handle.

INGREDIENTS

Quails	4–5, about 150 g each	Palm sugar (*gula Melaka*)	1$\frac{1}{2}$ Tbsp
		Thai fish sauce	2 Tbsp
Marinade		Light soy sauce	2 Tbsp
Ginger	2.5-cm knob, peeled and grated	Dry sherry	1 Tbsp
Garlic	4 cloves, peeled and chopped	Chinese five-spice powder	$\frac{1}{2}$ tsp
Shallots	2, peeled and chopped	Freshly ground black pepper	$\frac{1}{2}$ tsp

Sauce

Sugar	4 Tbsp
Red chilli	1, seeded and finely chopped
Garlic	1 clove, peeled and finely chopped
Water	125 ml
Thai fish sauce	5 Tbsp
Lime juice	4 Tbsp

METHOD

- Rinse quails inside and out then pat dry. With a large chef's knife, cut each in half through the breast and backbone then flatten by pressing on backbone.
- In a food processor, combine ginger, garlic, shallots and sugar into a paste. Add rest of marinade ingredients; process to combine.
- Transfer marinade to a shallow, non-reactive dish; add birds and turn to coat. Refrigerate covered for 4–12 hours, turning occasionally.
- Mash sugar, chilli and garlic into a paste. Transfer to a bowl and add water, fish sauce and lime juice. Stir until sugar is dissolved.
- Strain sauce and use immediately, or refrigerate tightly covered for up to 5 days.
- Place on grill or BBQ to cook. Brush sauce on quails and cook until charred. Serve with tamarind steak sauce* for the best effect.

*Tamarind Steak Sauce

Yields 500 ml

A salsa is a raw and chunky sauce. Here I am blending the sauce into a smooth purée but leaving a few tomatoes chunky to add to the texture. This sauce is Asian in origin although the concept of using salsas is either Mexican or South American.

INGREDIENTS

Tamarind purée	1 Tbsp
Water	125 ml
Tomatoes	250 g, peeled and chopped, with 3 left chunkier
Garlic	2 Tbsp, peeled and chopped
Shallots	120 g, peeled and chopped
Red chilli	1, seeded and sliced
Salt	to taste
Sugar	to taste

METHOD

- Mix tamarind purée with water and blend until mixture becomes thick. Drain off dregs and use 2 Tbsp of the thick liquid.
- To remove tomato skin, pour boiling water over tomatoes, cool then skin quickly with sharp knife.
- Combine remaining ingredients except half of the chopped tomatoes in a food processor. Process for about 3–4 minutes until smooth.
- Add remaining tomatoes and blend with tamarind purée. Refrigerate and use as desired.

Thai Chicken Breasts Cooked on the BBQ

Makes 20

Chicken breasts can be butterflied and stuffed with some filling before cooking. The result is sweet, moist and delicate chicken breasts.

INGREDIENTS

Lemon grass (*serai*)	2 stalks
Green chillies	3, seeded and chopped
Garlic	2 cloves, peeled and chopped
Spring onions (scallions)	3, chopped
Coriander (cilantro) leaves	1 handful
Coriander (cilantro) root	1
Freshly ground black pepper	1 tsp
Sugar	1 Tbsp
Salt	to taste
Lime zest	grated from 1 lime
Lime juice	4 Tbsp
Ginger	2-cm knob, peeled and grated
Thai fish sauce	1 Tbsp
Chicken breasts	4, skinned, deboned and butterflied

METHOD

- Remove and discard tough outer skin from lemon grass stalks and chop roughly. Place all ingredients, except chicken breasts, in a food processor and pulse until smooth.
- In a bowl, toss chicken with mixture. Refrigerate covered for 1 hour.
- Preheat BBQ. Barbecue or grill chicken, first over medium-hot coals until it is opaque with no trace of pink, for about 20 minutes. Turn over a few times until cooked, brushing with oil when necessary.
- Keep cooking until charred for the best effect with this recipe. Chicken may be served as entrées, finger food or picnic food using a light sauce made with 125 ml lime juice, 1 Tbsp grated palm sugar, 1 Tbsp chilli sauce and 1 Tbsp fish sauce.
- Mix well and use as sauce or toss this through a cucumber, carrot and chicken salad.

Middle-eastern Duck with Orange Glaze

Serves 6, with rice

INGREDIENTS
Glaze

Oranges	2, juiced and cooked with 3 pounded cloves
Soft honey or golden syrup	2 Tbsp
Duck breasts	3, with skin left on and scored
Ground clove and chinese five-spice powder	1 tsp
Orange rind	from 1 orange

METHOD
- Combine 3 Tbsp of orange juice with honey. Pour remaining orange juice into a shallow dish just wide enough for 3 breasts.
- Add duck breasts, skin side up. Cover and leave to marinate for 20 minutes at room temperature.
- This may be done up to 4 hours ahead of cooking, if the ducks are left to marinate in the refrigerator.
- For outdoor BBQ, grill over medium coals.
- Grill, skin side down, for 5 minutes, until skin is crispy. Baste with marinade throughout grilling. Turn and grill for further 8 minutes for medium-rare and 10 minutes for well-done.
- Cover with foil and leave to rest for 5 minutes before cutting diagonally into thin slices. Sprinkle with clove and five-spice powder and orange rind. Serve with garlic aioli sauce with coriander (see pg 45).

Note: As an alternative, you can make a Vietnamese sauce by combining 60 ml light soy sauce, 2 Tbsp dark soy sauce, 1 Tbsp *Hoisin* sauce and 1 Tbsp Chinese rice wine, adding chilli if desired.

Palm Sugar and Soy Wings

Makes 20

A recipe that helps to emphasise the fact that our recipes can be easily adapted. In this case, the wings can be marinated a few hours in advance, covered and refrigerated, then cooked slowly when required.

INGREDIENTS

Limes	2, juiced
Garlic	2 cloves, peeled and crushed
Chilli powder	1 Tbsp
Light soy sauce	1 Tbsp
Dark soy sauce	1 Tbsp
Palm sugar (*gula Melaka*)	1 Tbsp, melted in 2 Tbsp water in a microwave oven
Chicken wings	20, with tips cut off and bones jointed
Metal skewers	1 parallel pair
Salt	2 tsp
Rice flour	4 Tbsp

METHOD

- Combine lime juice, garlic, chilli powder, soy sauces and melted sugar in a bowl. Add wings and toss to coat evenly. Refrigerate covered for 2 hours, turning the wings every 30 minutes.
- Thread wings onto skewers. Sprinkle evenly with salt and dust lightly with rice flour.
- For outdoor BBQ, grill wings over medium-hot coals for 20-25 minutes, turning every 5 minutes, until the meat on the bone is opaque. Keep brushing with oil to complete cooking.
- For indoor grill, preheat grill. Arrange wings on a wire rack over an oven tray. Grill for 15–20 minutes. Turn once and cook until meat at the bone is opaque.
- Serve with tamarind steak sauce (see pg 57) or coconut *kemangi* sauce (see pg 9).

Note: Flour coating is not necessary but it prevents the wings from sticking to the plate.

Barbecued Fin (*Ikan Panggang Pari*)

Serves 4, when served with a meal

Grilling (*panggang*) is best done on a BBQ when fish is slow cooked with direct heat to give it the best flavour from the open fire. But it needs careful handling so keep a pair of tongs handy for turning the fish. Banana leaves make an aromatic base for the fish.

INGREDIENTS

Stingray (*pari*) or eagle ray fin, choose flatter fillets nearer the fins	500 g
Garlic	4 cloves, peeled
Spanish onion	1/2, peeled
Chilli paste	1 Tbsp
Lemon grass (*serai*)	2 stalks, blended
Ground turmeric	1/4 tsp
Prawn (shrimp) paste (*sambal belacan*)	1-cm piece, dry-roasted
Tamarind paste	1 Tbsp
Dried prawns (shrimps)	20 g, dry-roasted and pounded
Lime	1, juiced
Vegetable oil or olive oil	4 Tbsp
Sugar	to taste
Salt	to taste
Banana leaf or foil	

Garnish

Lime	1, juiced
Kaffir lime leaves	2, thinly sliced
Coconut cream	(optional) for drizzling

METHOD

- Cut stingray fillets into thin slices lengthways so that thin fillets are obtained. Blend remaining ingredients into a paste.
- Heat oil in a pan and fry blended ingredients, allowing paste to slowly mature on low heat.
- Place banana leaf and fish on oiled grill. Brush fried paste onto fish and grill or BBQ for 5 minutes. If the fins are thick, cook for another minute. Turn over and add more sauce and lime juice before taking off the BBQ.
- Snip off burnt edges of banana leaves, slide out fish from BBQ and serve on same banana leaf. Garnish with kaffir lime leaves and lime juice. Drizzle some coconut cream (optional).

Kanum Kluk

INGREDIENTS

Plain (all-purpose) flour	140 g
Coconut milk	400 ml
Egg	1
Sugar	a pinch
Salt	a pinch

Toppings

Dried prawns (shrimps) and chives	chopped
Dried chilli flakes	
Coconut flakes and nuts	chopped

Note: In Thai markets, you can find little clay moulds with shallow cup cake indentations with covers that look like padi hats. Or you may get cast-iron or aluminium trays with the same hollow indentations. Here we are using earthernware candle bowls – available in Indian homeware stores.

METHOD

- Whisk all ingredients in a bowl except for toppings. Whisk to a smooth batter.
- Heat candle bowl over low flame after oiling each one. When the bowl is heated, fill to the brim with coconut mixture and leave to cook slowly at the coolest end of the BBQ tray. Do not cook for too long or the coconut mixture will be too hard. Add some roasted dried shrimp just as coconut mixture is setting. Other toppings such as chives and chilli can also be used.
- Remove slowly and place on a dish.

Barbecued Kingfish and Pineapple Kebabs Served with Pineapple Rice

Makes about 12 kebabs

Cook the fish with just enough heat to ensure kebabs stay juicy. Overcooking will dry the fish.

INGREDIENTS

Kingfish cutlets or Spanish mackerel (*tenggiri*)	1 kg, skinned, deboned and with skin removed
Pineapple pieces	4, cubed

Marinade

Coriander (cilantro) leaves	4 Tbsp, ground
Garlic	2 cloves, peeled
Pineapple juice	2 Tbsp
Olive oil	2 Tbsp
Freshly ground black pepper	a pinch
Metal skewers	12

METHOD

- Cut fish into 2.5-cm cubes.
- Cube pineapple and thread into kebabs.
- Begin to thread fish kebabs, starting with a pineapple cube to secure the end. Thread on fish cubes, alternating with pineapple cubes and finally ending with a pineapple cube.
- Mix marinade ingredients then brush onto kebabs.
- Sprinkle generously with black pepper.
- Lightly brush barbecue plate or grill with oil and cook kebabs for 8 minutes, turning only once. Keep brushing with more oil and some marinade.
- Serve with pineapple rice*.

---

*Pineapple Rice

INGREDIENTS

Rice	450 g
Liquid	875 ml, half water and half pineapple juice
Salt	to taste
Thai sweet basil (*kemangi*) or mint	a handful
Green chilli	1, sliced for garnishing

METHOD

- Cook rice by absorption method and add Thai sweet basil just before removing.
- Garnish with sliced green chilli and serve with kebabs.

Charred Crab-stuffed Squid (*Sotong*)

Serves 4–6

The calamari is cleaned, stuffed and then charred carefully until the filling is firm. Since the filling is partially cooked, the calamari does not require much further cooking.

INGREDIENTS

Squid (*sotong*) tubes	4, each about 120 g, cleaned
Bamboo skewers	4, pre-soaked

Filling

Coriander (cilantro) leaves and root	100 g
Spring onions (scallions)	2
Lime peel	1 Tbsp
Chilli paste	1 tsp
Lemon grass (*serai*) bulb	1
Dried prawns (shrimps)	1 Tbsp
Canned crabmeat	125 g
Egg	1
Light soy sauce	1 Tbsp
Cooking oil	1 Tbsp

Basting liquid

Light soy sauce	1 Tbsp
Sesame oil	1 Tbsp
Vegetable oil or olive oil	1 Tbsp

METHOD

- Chop up coriander root.
- Blend all filling ingredients together. Shape into small sausages.
- Steam filling for 5 minutes to cook partially. Then stuff cooked filling into squid tubes and skewer at ends.
- Mix basting liquid ingredients together and brush squid.
- Place squid onto barbecue plate and brush generously with basting liquid.
- Cook for about 5–6 minutes. Baste with more oil if necessary. Don't cook too long or squid will become tough and dry. Besides, the filling is already cooked. If the squid is larger, allow for more filling and longer cooking time.
- Serve with garlic aioli sauce with coriander (see pg 47).

Fish Wrapped in Banana Leaves

Serves 6, when served with a meal

This is a recipe that is quite common in Malaysia but to make the cooking process unique, we now make it in a BBQ.

INGREDIENTS

Salt	to taste
Threadfin (*kurau*) fillets	500 g

Paste

Cumin	1 tsp, ground
Sugar	1 tsp or to taste
Dessicated coconut	150 g, with 1 Tbsp coconut cream
Green chillies	5, seeded
Mint and coriander leaves	8 Tbsp, chopped
Lime	1
Kitchen string	for tying
Banana leaves or foil	
Garlic	3 cloves, peeled and roughly chopped
Green, raw mango	1, small, or small green apple, roughly chopped with lime juice to keep it from darkening
Olive oil	2 Tbsp

METHOD

- Sprinkle salt on fish and place on a plate until needed.
- Blend all paste ingredients together. Apply paste liberally onto fillets and squeeze lime juice onto fish.
- Soften banana leaves in some hot water to make them pliant. Wipe them dry and wrap fish with chopped garlic and mango so that the leaves overlap well. Secure parcels with kitchen string.
- Barbecue fish on an oiled BBQ for 3 minutes on one side and then for about 2 minutes on the second side. The banana leaves will shrink a bit and char at the edges. You can open the leaves up if you want a charred effect.
- Carefully remove and serve each parcel partly opened on a platter with a garnish of mint or chilli "flowers" with a plain green mint chutney. Serve with rice or *roti*. (*Lavash* bread is the closest to *Naan.*)

Note: To make chilli "flowers", slice chillies into thin petals then dip them into ice-cold water to make them open up.

Sour Charcoal-grilled Prawns (*Gung Tien*)

Serves 4, with rice

The Thais have a fantastic array of fresh seafood that can be char-grilled, broiled or barbecued. When king prawns are grilled with a simple *Shao Hsing* marinade, the taste is unforgettable.

INGREDIENTS

King prawns (shrimps)   600 g

Marinade

Dark soy sauce	1 Tbsp
Shao Hsing wine	1 Tbsp
Lime	1, juiced

Dressing

Lime	1, juiced
Red chillies	3, finely chopped
Garlic	4 cloves, peeled and thinly sliced
Vietnamese mint (*daun kesum*)	1/2 cup, chopped into pieces
Thai fish sauce	2 Tbsp or to taste

Garnish

Fried onions	
Green mango	1, chopped

METHOD

- Clean prawns by removing feelers and using a pair of sharp scissors, cut through shell to devein prawns. This also allows marinade to penetrate into prawns.
- Combine marinade ingredients in a bowl.
- Brush marinade into prawn claws, making sure that fleshy areas are also brushed. You may have to do this a couple of times to make sure that the sauces penetrate.
- Grill prawns until shells start to turn red. Keep moving and turning prawns to distribute heat and to cook all over. Keep warm while dressing is being made.
- To make dressing, place some lime juice, chilli, garlic and chopped Vietnamese mint in a bowl and stir well. Add fish sauce to taste.
- Serve prawns with a fresh salad of greens such as cucumber, lettuce, spring onions, fried onions and green mango with dressing.

Char-grilled King Prawns (*Kung Kamraan Pla*)

Serves 2–3

The flesh of a king prawn is best cooked on a BBQ because of the fat content that helps to cook and grill the meat beautifully. However, the king prawn should be cleaned well and oiled before grilling. This makes the aromas quite unbeatable. Watch over carefully during grilling to avoid overcooking.

INGREDIENTS

King prawns (shrimps)	4, about 500 g
Butter	2 Tbsp
Cooking oil	1 Tbsp
Shallots	4, peeled and finely sliced

Marinade

Garlic	3 cloves, peeled
Kaffir lime leaves	3, with centre removed and leaves thinly sliced
Lemon grass (*serai*)	2 stalks, blended into paste

Sauce

Red chillies	10
Garlic	15 cloves, peeled
Lime juice	1 Tbsp
Thai fish sauce	2 Tbsp

Garnish

Thai sweet basil (*kemangi*)

METHOD

- Clean prawns. Brush shells and split backs open. Blend garlic, kaffir lime leaves and lemon grass then stuff into backs of prawns. Brush oil on the mixture.
- Melt butter and oil on the BBQ plate and sauté shallots for 30 seconds. Add shallots to cooking prawns.
- Use charcoal grill or BBQ plate to grill prawns, flesh side down, then turn after 6–7 minutes.
- Mix up ingredients for the sauce. Deseed chillies if you want it less spicy.
- Drizzle sauce on the platter and garnish with Thai basil.
- Serve with rice balls (see pg 39).

Orange *Tom Yum* Butterflied Prawns

Serves 6

The *tom yum* soup has flavours similar to our Laksa *assam* and can be adapted for other recipes. In this instance, it is used as a paste with the butterflied prawns. Once the paste is made, the rest is simple. It is a Thai dish that can be easily grilled or barbecued but again, care has to be taken to prevent over-grilling.

INGREDIENTS

Large king prawns (shrimps)	12

Marinade

Sherry or lime juice	4 Tbsp
Shallots	2, peeled and chopped
Freshly ground black pepper	1 tsp
Orange *tom yum* paste*	3 Tbsp
Bamboo skewers	12, pre-soaked
Rice flour	2 Tbsp
Sesame seeds	8 Tbsp, toasted
Cooking oil	4 Tbsp

METHOD

- Peel and devein prawns. Flatten backs so that they sit like butterflies, leaving tail shells intact.
- Combine sherry, shallots and pepper with *tom yum* paste in a tray. Brush marinade onto prawns and allow to sit in marinade for 2 hours.
- Thread prawns carefully onto bamboo skewers.
- Lay threaded prawns on the tray and brush once more with marinade. Roll prawns in some rice flour and then in sesame seeds, patting them on well. Refrigerate for 20 minutes before cooking.
- Brush BBQ plate lightly with oil, and place prawn kebabs on the plate. Allow to cook for about 2–3 minutes. Brush with marinade during cooking.
- Serve with fresh crusty herb rolls or with a light serving of chopped cucumber.
- White rice topped with orange *tom yum* paste can also be served.

*Orange *Tom Yum* Paste

INGREDIENTS

Red chillies	10 or less, seeded then chopped
Salt	1 tsp
Orange rind	from 1 orange
Outer layers of a peeled onion	3 Tbsp
Prawn (shrimp) paste (*sambal belacan*)	1 Tbsp, roasted
Rice vinegar	1 Tbsp
Palm sugar (*gula Melaka*)	1 tsp
Thai fish sauce	to taste
Orange	1, juiced

METHOD

- Pound all ingredients together. Brush on prawns then use as grilling marinade. Orange paste may also be used to flavour rice when it is being cooked.
- You may use the normal method of cooking rice and add some orange paste and salt to water before cooking rice. If desired, coconut milk can be added.

Threadfin (*Kurau*) Wrapped in Banana Leaves or Foil (*Patrani Maachi*)

Serves 4–6

This is a North Indian recipe that is normally cooked on a flat iron plate used for cooking *dhosai* or *chappati* but a BBQ does it much better so give it a try.

INGREDIENTS

Salt	to taste
Threadfin (*kurau*) fillets or whole fish	500 g

Paste

Cumin	1 tsp, ground
Sugar	1 tsp
Dessicated coconut	150 g, combined with 1 Tbsp coconut cream
Green chillies	5, seeded
Mint and coriander (cilantro) leaves	55 g, chopped
Olive oil	2 Tbsp
Lemon	1, juiced
Banana leaves or foil	
Garlic	3 cloves, peeled and chopped
Green, raw mango	1, or 1 green apple, chopped with lime juice to keep it from darkening

METHOD

- Sprinkle salt on fish and place on a plate until needed.
- Blend all paste ingredients together. Apply paste liberally onto fish fillets. Brush oil on fillets and squeeze lemon juice onto fish.
- Soften banana leaves in hot water to make them pliant then wipe dry and wrap fish with chopped garlic and mango so that the leaves overlap well.
- Secure parcels with kitchen string.
- Barbecue fish on a BBQ for 3 minutes on one side and then for about 2 minutes on the second side. The banana leaves will shrink a bit and char at the edges.
- Cover pan and cook on low for 5 minutes then carefully remove fish. Each parcel can be served partly opened on a platter with a garnishing of mint or chilli "flowers" (see pg 67) with a plain green mint chutney. Serve with rice or *roti*. (*Lavash* bread is the closest to *Naan*.)

Salmon Cooked in Lime, Lemon Grass and Garlic with Feta Cheese

Serves 4

Salmon may be an expensive fish in Asia but you can always substitute it with a fairly fatty fish like tuna or even carp.

INGREDIENTS

Salmon cutlets, tuna cutlets or carp cutlets	4, each about 150 g
Feta cheese or Indian *panir* or Cottage cheese	2 Tbsp

Marinade

Olive oil	1 Tbsp
Lime juice	125 ml
Lemon grass (*serai*)	3 stalks, thinly sliced then finely pounded
Garlic	1 clove, peeled, crushed and finely pounded

Garnish

Coriander (cilantro)	chopped
Lime zest	grated from 1 lime

METHOD

- To make marinade, mix oil, lime juice, lemon grass and garlic together.
- Brush marinade on each side of cutlet, then keep covered and refrigerated in marinade for about 2 hours.
- Prepare BBQ to medium heat and oil plate or grill. Place fillets over heat and cook on griddle or BBQ plate. Add olive oil to heated grill, place some marinade on grilling plate and brown until aromatic.
- Turn cutlets over, cover with more marinade and keep drizzling oil and marinade over fish. Squeeze lemon juice over fish and allow to cook a further 2 minutes for each piece.
- Place feta cheese on top of fish to melt and serve with salad of chopped coriander, sliced onions, lime juice and some olive oil. This barbecued fish goes especially well with some freshly cooked pasta or a bed of instant noodles drizzled with olive oil and coriander with salt to taste.

Note: Cheese is added only at the end after fish is cooked since it will melt on the BBQ. Fish will remain cooking after it is removed from BBQ, as heat cooks it from inside, so you can remove it when colour begins to change.

Silver Bream with Shallots

Serves 4

Fish such as bream or even threadfin can be cooked whole on a barbecue. Grilling on the barbecue will enhance its flavour, especially if the foil is removed towards the end of cooking and the fish is allowed to cook for a short time directly on the grill after being oiled.

INGREDIENTS

Silver bream	2, cut into halves
Shallots	10, peeled, washed and cut into strips
Ginger	5-cm knob, peeled and cut into strips
Kitchen foil	a large piece, cut into squares
Lemons	2, medium, juiced
Sesame oil	2 tsp

METHOD

- Score flesh through to bone, making four cuts at 2.5-cm intervals on both sides of each fish half.
- Press shallots and ginger strips into each cut.
- Lightly oil some foil and place fish halves individually on each foil square.
- Combine lemon juice and sesame oil and brush mixture lightly over each fish. Cover each fish half with another piece of foil and seal like an envelope.
- Place onto BBQ and cook over medium heat for about 6 minutes or until flesh starts to flake. Then remove foil and allow fish to cook directly on grill for a few minutes to crisp skin after oiling well.
- Serve with a salad of grated carrot and cucumber or pineapple drizzled with lime juice, fish sauce and palm sugar.

Note: To test if fish is cooked, flake the flesh near the head as this is the thickest part.

Squid on Mango Coconut Sauce

Serves 4

This dish can be served as an appetizer, salad or even as a main course.

The squid is a favourite in Malaysia but can be overcooked with too much grilling. It is best to prepare it just before serving by grilling it quickly with intense heat.

INGREDIENTS

Crabmeat	300 g
Coconut cream	2 Tbsp
Red onion	50 g, peeled and chopped
Dried wood ear fungus	10 g, soaked in warm water for 1 hour and cut into strips
Red chilli	1, seeded and diced
Thai sweet basil leaves (*kemangi*)	10, cut into strips
Egg white	from 1 egg
Salt	to taste
Baby squid (*sotong*) tubes	8 or 4 large squid, 120 g each, washed and with ink sac removed
Toothpicks	
Butter	

Garnish

Young coconut	120 g, scooped out with a spoon

METHOD

- Place crabmeat in a food processor with coconut cream. Blend until smooth.
- Put mixture in a cold bowl and stir in wood fungus, chilli, sweet basil leaves, onion and egg white. Mix well and season with salt.
- Fill squid with crab and fungus mixture. Secure opening with a toothpick.
- Brush squid with butter. Grill slowly on BBQ, turning as squid cooks. Allow about 6 minutes for each squid and turn after about 3 minutes. Brush on more butter as needed. Squid must be grilled or barbecued over medium heat but not for too long.
- Remove squid from BBQ and serve with mango coconut sauce and a green salad or rice. Garnish with young coconut.

Snapper with Mint and Beetroot

Serves 4–6

Simplicity is the key to cooking fish. In this case, the simple and popular technique produces a refreshing dish.

INGREDIENTS

Paste

Young ginger	3-cm knob, peeled and grated
Garlic	2 cloves, peeled and chopped
Red onion	1/2, peeled and blended

Lemon juice	1 1/2 Tbsp
Mint	55 g, chopped
Lime juice	2 Tbsp
Light soy sauce	2 tsp
Salt and black pepper	to taste
Large snapper or bream	1, about 2 kg, cleaned
Bamboo skewers	

Vegetables

Canned beetroot	1 can (250 g), drained and use 150 g of beetroot

METHOD

- Combine paste ingredients in a bowl. Mix well.
- Fill fish cavity with paste and secure with skewers.
- Place fish on lightly greased foil, and score fish three times on either side with a sharp knife before wrapping up fish in a parcel. You can also place fish on a greased barbecue plate or grill.
- Cook fish on BBQ for about 30–35 minutes or until flesh flakes easily. Keep oiling fish by spraying evenly with oil using a olive oil spray or a brush.
- Serve with sliced beetroot and sour cream, and a tossed green salad.

Mango Coconut Sauce (Sauce *Mangga*)

Yields 125 ml

INGREDIENTS

Mango flesh	120 g
Young coconut flesh	60 g
Lime juice	1 Tbsp, freshly squeezed
Salt	to taste

METHOD

- Put mango, coconut and lime juice in a food processor and process until silky.
- Remove from food processor and season with salt. Heat sauce.

Note: Mango spoils easily so prepare this sauce only when required.

Tandoori *Maach*

Serves 4–6

This North Indian Tandoor paste, when applied onto fish, not only gives the fish flavour but also prevents the fish from drying out as it protects the delicate flesh.

INGREDIENTS

Red snapper	1.5–2 kg or 4 x 180–200 g bass (yellow grouper) cutlets, cleaned
Cooking oil	2 tsp
Banana leaves or foil	2 pieces

Tandoori paste

Coriander seeds	1 Tbsp
Lime juice	3 Tbsp
Salt	1/4 tsp
Garlic	6 cloves, peeled
Ginger	5-cm knob, peeled
Turmeric powder	1 tsp
Garam masala	1 tsp
Chilli paste	2 tsp or to taste
Tamarind paste	1 Tbsp
Lime juice	to taste

METHOD

- To make paste, dry-roast coriander seeds, blend then add remaining ingredients and blend well, grinding until all spices are smooth. You may have to add a few drops of water.
- Assemble fish cutlets on banana leaf and brush with oil. Cover all over with paste. Place onto a preheated and oiled BBQ plate.
- Cook fish for 40 minutes or until flesh is flaky but moist. Turn fish and press more paste into cutlets halfway through cooking time.
- Remove fish and place on a plate. Scrape remains of paste that have been left on BBQ plate and place on fish.
- Serve with *roti* or rice.

Sour Star Fruit (*Belimbing*) Sauce

Yields 400 ml

The finger star fruit (*belimbing*) has a flavour unmatched and works well in a sauce for meats.

INGREDIENTS

Vegetable oil or olive oil	1 Tbsp
Red onion	1, peeled and chopped
Garlic	2 cloves, peeled and diced
Ginger	3-cm knob, peeled and diced
Lemon grass (*serai*)	1 stalk, diced
Prawn (shrimp) paste (*sambal belacan*)	2 tsp
Finger star fruit (*belimbing*)	200 g
Candlenuts	2
Ground turmeric	1 tsp
Chilli sauce	1 Tbsp, mixed with 1 Tbsp water
Coconut milk	375 ml
Salt	to taste

METHOD

- Heat oil in a saucepan. Sauté onion, garlic, ginger and lemon grass in hot oil for 2 minutes without browning. Drain off oil.
- Add prawn paste and finger star fruit. Add candlenuts and ground turmeric into saucepan and sauté for 2 minutes until aromatic.
- Pour in chilli sauce and coconut milk and add salt to taste. Simmer for 7–10 minutes.
- Blend everything in a food processor until smooth and then brush onto fish or prawns while barbecuing.

Green Chilli Sauce

Yields 625 ml

This is a mild green chilli sauce that goes well with fish and barbecues. Dried prawns add texture to this simple sauce.

INGREDIENTS

Olive oil or vegetable oil	1 Tbsp
Shallots	100 g, peeled and diced
Garlic	1¹/₂ Tbsp, peeled and diced
Greater galangal	1¹/₂ Tbsp, peeled and diced
Ginger	1¹/₂ Tbsp, peeled and diced
Lemon grass (*serai*)	3 stalks, blended
Turmeric leaf	¹/₂, finely shredded
Dried prawns (shrimps)	2 tsp, dry-roasted and pounded
Green tomatoes or green mango	2, chopped
Green chillies	3–5, seeded
Coconut milk	250 ml

METHOD

- Heat oil in a saucepan. Add shallots, garlic, galangal, ginger, lemon grass and turmeric leaf. Sauté until light brown.
- Add in dried prawns, tomatoes and chillies and sauté for a further 2–3 minutes.
- Pour in coconut milk and bring mixture to the boil. Simmer for about 5 minutes to thicken.
- Remove from heat and discard lemon grass. Blend in a food processor for 2–4 minutes until smooth.
- Serve as a sauce for fish.

Coriander (Cilantro) Chilli Butter

Yields 10–15 servings

A novel way of using coriander is to make it into a paste with butter for meats or fish in a barbecue recipe. This adds maturity to any fish or meat and it is particularly good with lamb.

INGREDIENTS

Unsalted butter	250 g, softened
Coriander (cilantro) leaves	100 g, chopped
Green chillies	2, seeded and chopped
Lime juice	1 Tbsp
Salt	2 tsp
Freshly ground black pepper	1 tsp

METHOD

- Place all ingredients in a food processor; pulse until well blended. Place in freezer for about 45 minutes or until it hardens. Roll into a cigar shape and wrap with some cling film, twisting both ends to secure.
- To serve, warm knife under hot water then slice butter into 1-cm pieces and place on meat for barbecuing together.
- After slicing, always re-wrap unused portion tightly with cling film before returning to freezer. To keep sliced coriander butter ready for use when outdoors, place in a bowl of cold water.

Ginger BBQ Glaze for Pork, Lamb or Beef Ribs

Yields 250 ml

Brushing this over barbecued or char-grilled pork, grilled ribs, or grilled ham produces a different flavour from a spicy sweet glaze. Heat before use.

INGREDIENTS

Instant coffee powder	1 Tbsp
Boiling water	1 tsp
Ginger wine or squeezed ginger juice	125 ml
Palm sugar (*gula Melaka*)	125 g, shaved fine and firmly packed
Ginger	2 tsp, peeled and ground
Dry mustard	1/2 tsp

METHOD

- Dissolve coffee powder with boiling water. Mix all ingredients by whisking together. Simmer over low heat for 5–10 minutes.
- While glaze is still warm, brush over meat during the last 15 minutes of grilling to prevent the sugar in it from burning.
- A good way to prevent such charring is to coat meat with a thin soy marinade when you start grilling. Only add glaze when meat is partially cooked.

Cumin and Curry Powder Rub

For about 1 kg fish or prawns

INGREDIENTS

Ground cumin	2 tsp
Chilli powder	1 tsp
Mustard seeds	2 tsp, semi-pounded
Tamarind paste	1 Tbsp
Olive oil or vegetable oil	2 Tbsp
Turmeric powder	a pinch

METHOD

- Mix all ingredients together in a bowl, using oil to facilitate blending.
- Brush onto fish and peeled prawns, allowing to marinate for 3–4 hours.
- Leave to refrigerate then grill or barbecue, basting with a bit of the mix and more oil.

Note: When using marinade to bast meat for the BBQ, cook the marinade first to kill off the bacteria. Simply microwave on high for 2 minutes.

Wasabi *Miso* Sauce for Steak Tartare or Quickly Barbecued Beef

Yields 125 ml

Usually, the sauce for a rare steak should be light so that the meat flavours are retained. Here the wasabi and *miso* combination is strong but it combines well, especially with barbecued beef.

INGREDIENTS

Miso	4 Tbsp
Runny honey	4 Tbsp
Creamy wasabi sauce	1 Tbsp, from tube
Ginger	2 Tbsp, peeled and grated
Garlic	2 cloves, peeled and crushed
Light soy sauce	2 Tbsp
Rice wine	2 Tbsp

METHOD

- Combine all ingredients until smooth. Cover and stand for 30 minutes at room temperature for flavours to blend.
- Serve at room temperature. Best eaten with a lightly cooked, rare barbecued beef steak or with salmon grilled on the BBQ.

Note: Wasabi sauce is available in tube form at supermarkets.

Moroccan Spice Rub

Yields 125 g

The Middle Easterners have their own spice flavourings. Although they use some of our herbs and spices, the way in which they are used is extraordinary. *Soumac*, a sour berry, may not be available but the Indian *kokum* (a sour fruit) or tamarind can be an effective substitute.

This blend is perfect on 2 kg of chicken, lamb ribs or kebabs.

INGREDIENTS

Cumin	2 Tbsp, dry-roasted and ground
Ground turmeric	1 tsp
Cinnamon	2 tsp, ground
Black pepper	1 Tbsp, ground
Soumac	1 tsp or 2 pieces *kokum*
Chilli powder	$1/2$ tsp
Coarse salt	2 tsp

METHOD

- Mix spices and grind together after warming slightly in a dry pan.
- Combine all ingredients in a small dish. Store in an airtight container at room temperature.
- Rub on meat, especially on beef steaks or lamb ribs and brush with lime juice. Refrigerate covered for 2 hours, then grill or barbecue.

Herb Salsa

Yields 80 ml

This sauce is good with fish.

INGREDIENTS

Red chilli	1, seeded and roughly cut
Coriander (cilantro)	1 bunch
Parsley	1 bunch
Capers	1 Tbsp
Garlic	2 cloves, peeled and roughly chopped
Extra virgin olive oil	2 Tbsp

METHOD

- Combine all ingredients in a food processor. Process in short bursts, scraping down the sides, until finely chopped. Serve in a separate bowl.

Tomato Based Marinade

For about 600 g–1 kg meat

INGREDIENTS
Garlic	4 cloves, diced
Tomato purée	100 g
Olive oil	100 g
Red wine or *Shao Hsing* wine	125 ml
Dried oregano or fresh Thai sweet basil (*kemangi*)	1 Tbsp

METHOD
• Follow the previous recipe.

Marinade for Seafood

Lime Based Marinade

For about 500 g seafood

INGREDIENTS
Lime juice	150 g
Orange juice	150 g
Olive oil	100 g
Garlic	3 cloves, peeled and diced
Chilli paste	1 tsp or to taste
Palm sugar	50 g, finely shaved

METHOD
• Mix ingredients in a bowl and whisk well with a non-metal whisk.
• Place seafood in marinade; rub into seafood. Turn to coat after a couple of hours and leave seafood to marinate in the refrigerator for 3–4 hours.
• Remove seafood from marinade and discard liquid.

Marinades for Lamb, Beef and Goat

The difference between a marinade and a sauce is that the marinade allows the meat to sit in it while it acts as a tenderiser. A meat marinade may be slightly heavier than a quick fish marinade that does not require any tenderising.

Chinese Five-spice Marinade

For about 1 kg meat

INGREDIENTS
Thin soy sauce	100 g
Thick soy sauce	100 g
Sesame oil	1 tsp
Minced ginger	1 Tbsp
Minced garlic	1 Tbsp
Honey	1 Tbsp
Shao Hsing wine or dry sherry	1 Tbsp
Chinese five-spice powder	2 tsp

METHOD
• Mix ingredients in a bowl and whisk.
• Place meat in marinade; rub into meat. Turn to coat after a couple of hours and leave meat in marinade for up to 10 hours.
• Remove meat from marinade and discard liquid.

BBQ Essentials

Exact grilling times are difficult to predict, especially when cooking outdoors. Fires burn differently under different conditions and factors such as wind and temperature make outdoor cooking more like guesswork rather than an exact science. Trust your senses and watch the meat closely to prevent overcooking. Meat, when overcooked, can be dry and devoid of all its moisture.

Notes

- Do not salt any meat until after it is cooked.
- Thinner pieces need more care since they lose their juices more easily.
- Piercing meat then adding pastes helps to give flavours. Avoid piercing too much or juices will be lost.
- BBQ times are given with emphasis on whether an outdoor BBQ or an indoor Hibachi grill are used. The times are varied and need adjusting.

General Barbecuing

For outdoor BBQ, grill over medium-hot coals.
For indoor grill or Hibachi grill, preheat ridged cast-iron pan over high heat.

3 minutes per side – rare
4 minutes per side – medium rare
5 minutes per side – well done

Butterfly Technique

When butterflying meat with bone, such as leg of lamb, start by placing meat on a cutting board, skin side down. Cut around exposed bone at the wide end of the leg. Cut the bone free at the joint and detach. Cut a slit along the length of the bone to expose and loosen. Use short and shallow cuts and scrape with the knife blade to release the meat from the bone. Remove bone.

Make a lengthwise slit along the thick section of the meat next to the cavity left by the bone. Open out the flap and spread the meat flat out like a book. Make another horizontal cut in the thick meat opposite and open out flat to form a "butterfly" shape with the entire piece.

When butterflying meat without bone, slice three-quarters down the centre of the width of the meat and open out flat to form a "butterfly" shape.

Beef

Marbled beef (beef with fat spread in between) cooks well as the fat released adds flavour. It only needs a light brush of oil and some marinade before grilling.

To Test if Meat is Done

Use your finger to touch test for doneness. The meat should feel soft, firm and juicy to the touch.

Resting

For juicy, tender beef, always allow meat to relax and let the juices settle inside meat before serving. Cover loosely with foil to keep warm and let it stand for 5 minutes.

Final Flavouring

Salting meat or fish before cooking draws out tasty juices and toughens the flesh, so always add seasoning just before serving, not before cooking.

Poultry

With poultry, the meat should look opaque and juicy.

Pork

Pork cooks well as its fat content makes it juicy and gives the finished dish aroma and enticing flavour. Always make sure that pork is cooked thoroughly.

Fish

Fish should not be overcooked as it is a delicate meat. Test fish by slicing through the thickest part with a knife. It should not be opaque but remain white, juicy and flaky.

Touch Test for Meat

To test if meat is cooked, there is a simple touch test. The feel of the various degrees of doneness of meat correspond closely to the feel of the fleshy part of your palm below your thumb.

Press the meat with your finger then compare with the feel of the fleshy part of your palm below your thumb on your other hand. This has to be done while your thumb is touching another finger since the muscle in the fleshy part of your palm tenses and becomes progressively more resistant.

For rare: have your thumb touching your index finger
For medium-rare: have your thumb touching your middle finger
For medium: have your thumb touching your third finger
For well-done: have your thumb touching your little finger

Fork Test for Fish

Use a fork to prick the fish gently. When it is done, you will find the flesh firm, just beginning to flake and opaque through the centre but still moist. This moistness is part of the cooking process and the fish will continue cooking when taken off the grill, so do not leave it on the grill for too long or it will dry up and spoil.

GLOSSARY

Greater galangal

Lemon grass

Coriander (cilantro)

Kaffir lime leaves

Cucumber

Aubergine (eggplant)

Aubergine (eggplant)
Originating from Asia, the aubergine comes in different shapes, sizes and colours, with a surprising variation in flavour. Garden aubergines vary considerably in shape, size and colour – from smallish spheres of white, pale green, white streaked with purple, mauve and shades of yellow to rich, deep purple specimens that weigh around 1 kg. Aubergine is popular in China, Japan, India, Indonesia, Malaysia, the Philippines, Sri Lanka and Thailand.

Pea aubergines grow in clusters of tiny spheres with a tough skin and bitter taste. They are used whole in curries in Malaysia *(terung pipit)*, Indonesia *(terokak)* and Thailand *(makhua puang)* and eaten raw with *nam prik* (sauce or dip) in Thailand.

Capsicum (bell pepper)
Capsicums are also called bell peppers because of their bell-like shape. They are a kind of sweet pepper with a mild, sweet flavour and very juicy flesh. There are green, red, yellow, orange, brown and purple ones. Red capsicums are simply vine-ripened green capsicums that have ripened longer, so they are very sweet. Always choose firm ones, with richly coloured, shiny skin and that are heavy for their size. Avoid limp, shrivelled ones or those with soft or bruised spots. To store capsicums properly, keep in a plastic bag and refrigerate for up to a week.

Chillies
Native to Mexico, chillies are now available in many forms: fresh, dried, powdered, flaked, as well as in the form of sauces, *sambals* and paste. They range from mild to wild, and the smaller the chilli the hotter it is. Chillies are used either unripe, when they are green, or ripe, after they turn red. Ripe chillies are usually pounded or ground into a paste, chopped or used whole for flavouring or cut into various shapes for garnishing. Both red and green chillies are also available pickled. Dried chillies are pounded or ground and used for flavouring and seasoning.

Coriander (cilantro)
Also known as Chinese parsley, coriander leaves have a strong flavour and are used for flavouring and garnishing food. It should not be used as a substitute for English parsley except for garnishing. Coriander leaves are commonly used in Indian, Mexican, Caribbean and Asian cuisine.

Cucumber
Ancient cultivated vegetables believed to be indigenous to India, cucumbers come in many varieties, shapes and sizes. Available all year round, they are usually eaten raw in salads. They can also be bought pickled.

Curry leaves
Sprigs of small, shiny, pointed leaves with a distinctive fragrance, curry leaves are used most frequently in south India , Sri Lanka, Malaysia and Singapore and Fiji. Fresh curry leaves are normally sautéed with onions while making curry. Dried curry leaves, which are probably easier to find in Western countries, are not as strongly flavoured, but they serve the purpose.

Curry leaves

Garlic

Capsicum (bell pepper)

Kaffir lime and lemon

Chillies

Galangal

Greater galangal, called *lengkuas* in Malaysia or *laos* in Indonesia, is native to Malaysia and Java. It has a delicate flavour and is normally used fresh in cooking. Dried or ground galangal can also be used. In a recipe, 1 Tbsp chopped fresh galangal is equivalent to 1 tsp ground galangal.

Lesser galangal or aromatic ginger, called *cekur* in Malaysia and Singapore or *kencur* in Indonesia, is a smaller variety of galangal. It has a stronger flavour, and therefore only a small quantity needs to be used. In a recipe, 1 tsp chopped lesser galangal is equivalent to 1/2 tsp ground lesser galangal.

Garlic

Garlic belongs to the lily family, together with spring onion, chive, leek and shallot. The garlic bulb is the edible part and it is made up of individual cloves, each encased in its own whitish skin. When choosing garlic, pick firm and plump bulbs with dry skins. To store fresh garlic properly, keep them in an open container and leave in a cool, dark place. Unbroken bulbs will keep for up to 8 weeks while individual cloves will only keep for 3–10 days.

Kaffir lime

Also known as *limau purut* in Malaysia and *makrut* in Thailand, the kaffir lime is a small pear-shaped citrus fruit grown in Southeast Asia. It has bumpy and wrinkled skin that is yellow-green in colour. The juice is seldom used in cooking but the skin, with its high concentration of aromatic oils, is an essential ingredient for preparing Thai curry pastes. The grated zest is used to impart a piquant flavour.

Kaffir lime leaves

These leaves, called *daun limau purut* in Malaysia, are from the kaffir lime plant. The leaves are commonly used fresh or dried in curries for a slightly delicate lemony flavour. Sometimes, they are finely shredded and added to salads or cooked food. A suitable substitute is the tender new leaves of the lemon or grapefruit.

Lemon

Native to India, the lemon is the most versatile of all citrus fruit. It takes just a few drops of lemon juice to enhance the flavour of delicate fish or poultry dishes, creams and pies. The acid in the juice also prevents certain types of cut fruit from turning brown when exposed to air.

Lemon grass

Lemon grass, a long lemon-scented grass known as *serai* in Malaysia and Singapore, is popular for flavouring curries and soups. Only the pale lower portions of the stem, with the tough outer layers peeled away, is used for cooking. If lemon grass is not available, two or three strips of thinly peeled lemon zest can be used as a substitute.

Red onion

Sweet potato

Lotus root

Potato

Yam bean

Lotus root

Lotus root is an underwater root that grows as long as 1.2 m. It has a reddish-brown skin that has to be peeled off prior to using. The lotus root's creamy-white flesh has the crisp texture of a raw potato and a flavour akin to fresh coconut. It is available canned, dried or candied and can be used raw, or even candied, in salads, stir-fries and soups. as a vegetable or in dessert dishes.

Papaya (paw paw)

Indigenous to Central America, papayas range in size from very small to very large, and they are eaten both green and ripe. When ripe, the papaya has soft, juicy flesh and a fairly sweet taste (similar to apricot) and makes a good dessert or breakfast fruit. The unripe fruit, which has crisp, firm flesh, can be cooked as a vegetable and is also used to make preserves and pickles.

The fruit is very popular in Asia, where the flowers, leaves and young stems of the papaya tree are also cooked and eaten.

Pineapple

Native to South America, the pineapple is really a cluster of fruits of the Ananas tree that combine to form one 'multiple fruit'. The pineapple is one of the most popular of all tropical fruit. Available all year round, it makes an excellent dessert fruit. It can be bought fresh or canned. The fruit is delicious eaten ripe. In Asia, semi-ripe pineapple is used in sour soups and curries.

Potato

Potatoes are the world's most popular tuber and are available in hundreds of varieties including russet, long white and red. Different types of potatoes are good for different ways of preparation. Russet potatoes are best for baking and frying whereas others such as red potatoes are best for boiling. When choosing potatoes, pick firm ones with tight unblemished skin, having no sprouts or green areas. Always store potatoes in a cool dark area and do not refrigerate, as the cold temperatures will convert the starches into sugars, creating a dark potato.

Red onion

This type of onion is medium to large in size and is mild and sweet in flavour. It has purplish red skin and is white on the inside.

Papaya (paw paw)

Pineapple

Vietnamese mint (*kesum*) leaves

Thai sweet basil leaves (*kemangi*)

Starfruit

Star fruit

There are five definitive ribs that traverse the length of the star fruit which gives it its star-like shape, hence its name. It grows well in tropical climates. The star fruit has a thin and glossy golden-yellow skin and translucent flesh. The star fruit becomes very juicy and fragrant when ripened. Its flavour ranges from exotically sweet to refreshingly tart, depending on the variety of star fruit. To pick sweet star fruit, choose the firm ones with ribs set far apart and with bright and even colour. Use ripe star fruit within a few days or store, wrapped tightly in a plastic bag, in the refrigerator for up to a week. Star fruit can be used unpeeled in salads, desserts or as a garnish.

Sweet potato

This large edible root belongs to the morning-glory family and is native to the tropical areas of the Americas. The pale-skinned sweet potato has a thin, light yellow skin and a pale yellow flesh. Its flavour is not sweet and after being cooked, the pale sweet potato is dry and crumbly, much like a white baking potato. When buying fresh sweet potatoes, choose small to medium-sized ones with smooth, unbruised skins. Sweet potatoes don't keep well unless stored in a dry and dark place. Then they can be stored for 3–4 weeks. Otherwise, store in a cool, dark place and use within a week of purchase. Do not refrigerate. Sweet potatoes are high in vitamins A and C.

Thai sweet basil leaves (*kemangi*)

Called *bai horapa* in Thai, Thai sweet basil has lush, deep green leaves, purplish flower buds and stems and carries anise overtones to its sweet basil scent. The flower buds are also edible, adding a wonderful floral bouquet.

Vietnamese mint (*kesum*) leaf

The narrow, pointed Vietnamese mint leaves are not a variety of mint. The leaves are an essential ingredient in the famous Singaporean/Malaysian seafood noodle soup, laksa, and are therefore known in Malaysia and Singapore as *daun laksa* (laksa leaf) or *daun kesum*.

Yam bean

Also known as *sng kuang* or *bung kuang*, this is a common edible tuber originally from South America but grows well in Southeast Asia. It is a favourite vegetable that can be cooked or used raw. Crunchy strips of the vegetable are the main ingredient in Malaysian *popiah*, spring rolls and *rojak*.

WEIGHTS & MEASURES

Quantities for this book are given in Metric and American measures. Standard spoon and cup measurements used are: 1 tsp = 5 ml, 1 dsp = 10 ml, 1 Tbsp = 15 ml, 1 cup = 250 ml.
All measures are level unless otherwise stated.

LIQUID AND VOLUME MEASURES

Metric	Imperial	American
5 ml	$^1/_6$ fl oz	1 tsp
10 ml	$^1/_3$ fl oz	1 dsp
15 ml	$^1/_2$ fl oz	1 Tbsp
60 ml	2 fl oz	$^1/_4$ cup (4 Tbsp)
85 ml	$2^1/_2$ fl oz	$^1/_3$ cup
90 ml	3 fl oz	$^3/_8$ cup (6 Tbsp)
125 ml	4 fl oz	$^1/_2$ cup
180 ml	6 fl oz	$^3/_4$ cup
250 ml	8 fl oz	1 cup
300 ml	10 fl oz ($^1/_2$ pint)	$1^1/_4$ cups
375 ml	12 fl oz	$1^1/_2$ cups
435 ml	14 fl oz	$1^3/_4$ cups
500 ml	16 fl oz	2 cups
625 ml	20 fl oz (1 pint)	$2^1/_2$ cups
750 ml	24 fl oz ($1^1/_5$ pints)	3 cups
1 litre	32 fl oz ($1^3/_5$ pints)	4 cups
1.25 litres	40 fl oz (2 pints)	5 cups
1.5 litres	48 fl oz ($2^2/_5$ pints)	6 cups
2.5 litres	80 fl oz (4 pints)	10 cups

DRY MEASURES

Metric	Imperial
30 g	1 ounce
45 g	$1^1/_2$ ounces
55 g	2 ounces
70 g	$2^1/_2$ ounces
85 g	3 ounces
100 g	$3^1/_2$ ounces
110 g	4 ounces
125 g	$4^1/_2$ ounces
140 g	5 ounces
280 g	10 ounces
450 g	16 ounces (1 pound)
500 g	1 pound, $1^1/_2$ ounces
700 g	$1^1/_2$ pounds
800 g	$1^3/_4$ pounds
1 kg	2 pounds, 3 ounces
1.5 kg	3 pounds, $4^1/_2$ ounces
2 kg	4 pounds, 6 ounces

OVEN TEMPERATURE

	℃	℉	Gas Regulo
Very slow	120	250	1
Slow	150	300	2
Moderately slow	160	325	3
Moderate	180	350	4
Moderately hot	190/200	370/400	5/6
Hot	210/220	410/440	6/7
Very hot	230	450	8
Super hot	250/290	475/550	9/10

LENGTH

Metric	Imperial
0.5 cm	$^1/_4$ inch
1 cm	$^1/_2$ inch
1.5 cm	$^3/_4$ inch
2.5 cm	1 inch

ABBREVIATION

tsp	teaspoon
Tbsp	tablespoon
g	gram
kg	kilogram
ml	millilitre